D1479269

Blooming in the Desert

Blooming in the Desert

Favorite Teachings
of the Wildflower Monk
Taungpulu Tawya Kaba-Aye Sayadaw Phaya

Edited by
Anne Teich

North Atlantic Books
Berkeley, California

Blooming in the Desert:
Favorite Teachings of the Wildflower Monk Taungpulu Sayadaw

Published by
North Atlantic Books
P.O. Box 12327
Berkeley, California 94712

Distributed to the book trade by Publishers Group West.

Cover and book design by Legacy Media, Inc.
Cover photograph of Taungpulu Sayadaw by Joseph Baxter.
Photographs courtesy of the Sircar family and Anne Teich.
Photo captions from *The Dhammapada*, translated by Narada Maha Thera (Calcutta: Maha Bodhi Society of India, 1962).

Blooming in the Desert: Favorite Teachings of the Wildflower Monk Taungpulu Sayadaw is sponsored in part by the Society for the Study of Native Arts and Sciences, a nonprofit educational corporation whose goals are to develop an educational and crosscultural perspective linking various scientific, social, and artistic fields; to nurture a holistic view of the arts, sciences, humanities, and healing; and to publish and distribute literature on the relationship of mind, body, and nature.

Library of Congress Cataloguing-in Publication Data
Nandiya Mather , A rhan .
    Blooming in the Desert : favorite teachings of the wildflower monk / Taungpulu Tawya Kaba-Aye Sayadaw Phaya ; edited by Anne Teich
      p. cm.
    ISBN 1-55643-223-2 (paper)
    1. Buddhism—Doctrines. 2. Buddhism—Burma. I. Teich, Anne. II. Title. III. Title: Blooming in the desert
BQ4165.N355 1996
294.3'42—dc20   96-12371
                                                                      CIP

1 2 3 4 5 6 7 8 9 / 00 99 98 97 96

With gratitude to my parents
Richard John and Anna Maud
for their love and sacrifice
on my behalf

Contents

༄

Foreword

Andrew Harvey

ᧂ

In the *Dhammapada* the Buddha said:

> The thoughtful exert themselves; they do not relish attach-
> ment. Like swans leaving a lake, they abandon one attach-
> ment after another. For one who is docile as the earth, a
> pillar of good conduct, like an unpolluted lake, there are no
> more compulsive routines.... the thought is calm, the action
> and speech are calm, in one who is liberated and gone to
> serenity by perfect knowledge.

I never had the grace to meet or receive teachings directly from
Taungpulu Sayadaw, but everything I have heard about him—
and over the years I have been told many stories about his gra-
ciousness and powers of instruction and healing—convince me that
in this frail, unpretentious figure from Burma, modern Buddhism
produced an authentically holy being, one whose life and teaching
continue to convey to anyone who comes to learn about them
the humble nobility of the Theravadin ideal, whose "thought,
speech, and action" had the calm the Buddha praised, and whose
personality emanated the luminous joy of one who is "liberated
and gone to serenity by perfect knowledge."

When Anne Teich writes in her Introduction to the Sayadaw's
teachings that "Just seeing him was a powerful teaching in the benefits of living a simple, strenuous life of renunciation," I believe
her; when Taungpulu died in 1986 at the age of 91, he was mourned
by his entire world, by rich and poor alike, by generals and gov-
ernment officials and sweepers and near-destitute farmers. For over

half a century, like the Buddha himself, the Sayadaw was a living sign of the truth of the Holy Dharma, a proof that its teachings and practices really can create beings of illumined and active compassion. For many Burmese who had to flee the military dictatorship in Burma, just knowing that Taungpulu Sayadaw was still alive in the country they had been forced to abandon provided hope and inspiration for the future. In his person, Sayadaw symbolized for them—and symbolizes still—everything that was sacred in old Burma, all the simplicity, fervor, and spiritual grace of a rapidly vanishing and menaced civilization.

In 1978, at the age of eighty, Taungpulu Sayadaw left his homeland for the first time to come to the United States at the invitation of his senior student, Dr. Rina Sircar. During four subsequent visits he changed many lives by his teaching and by what one Western disciple has described to me as the "almost shocking stillness and humility of his presence." Now, in this book, a representative selection of the Sayadaw's teachings are available for the first time.

All great teachers have their own personality and it is one of the joys of this fine selection that Taungpulu's spiritual personality should be so clearly revealed throughout in all its shrewdness, wit, hard-headed noble realism, and deep natural compassion for the suffering of all sentient beings. Decades of arduous self-discipline and of teaching all kinds of people in all kinds of situations honed in Taungpulu Sayadaw the vivid purity and clarity that are everywhere evident in these pages. There is nothing at all sentimental or fuzzy-edged about either the Sayadaw or the austerely unillusioned tradition that shaped him—and in an age like ours where soft opinions and self-aggrandizing spiritual theories are freely touted, and an inability to confront calmly the true tragic facts of existence is all too apparent, such a personality and such teachings have the bracing and refreshing power of a clear and cooling mountain stream.

One of the enduring strengths of the Theravada Buddhist tradition is that like its founder the Buddha, it treats human beings as adults capable of hearing and absorbing fiercely unflattering clarities in the pursuit of liberation. This is a tradition that never pretends that spiritual transformation is easily or cheaply won, that knows an immense and incessant effort of meditation and loving service is required for any authentic spiritual progress to be made, and that the price of growing toward awakening is continual vigilance and a continually renewed humble commitment to truth. The teachings of Taungpulu Sayadaw represent this tradition at its most naked and challenging; you will not find anything in them that coddles the false self or provides anything but the most realistic consolation.

For me, the most remarkable single aspect of the Sayadaw's teachings and of the tradition they derive from is their astonishing psychological penetration. The Buddha said in the *Dhammapada*, "Everything has mind in the lead, has mind in the forefront, is made by mind"; the greatness of the Theravada tradition lies, I believe, in the precision of its attention to "mind," its meticulously unshrinking and accurate analysis of how "mind" works and how the mindstream has to be continually purified and kept stable by an unflinching practice of mindfulness. The actual meditative practices that arise from such a concentration—practices of breathing, noting, and walking—have no equal in any spiritual tradition for efficiency and efficacy. These practices provide a fundamental hygiene of spirit; they should be learned by everyone, whatever path they are on.

Consider, for example, what the Sayadaw has to tell us about greed and grasping of all kinds:

> The more we get, the more we want. Greed is like a wild animal; if you feed a wild animal you cannot drive him away. Even though you try to drive him away with sticks and stones,

he will not go away. So it is with greed. If we "feed" sensual pleasures to the wild animal of greed, it will never go away, it will become stronger and stronger.

After such a fierce analysis one could be forgiven for expecting an even fiercer solution; Taungpulu's answer is however both wise and kind and exemplifies the cool pragmatic intelligence of Theravada Buddhism. For him, the solution to greed does not lie in self-hatred, penance, or any kind of morbid fear of the self's impulses (which could lead to a subtle obsession with the very false self that is at the root of all suffering); it lies in the consistent, persistent, gently merciless application of analysis of the facts of existence, which reveals the hollowness of all "goals" except that of attaining liberation. Taungpulu tells us:

> The best way to deal with greed is to see it as impermanent, to see that it doesn't really bring happiness, and to see that pleasures are not substantial, not "I," "me," or "mine."

He adds:

> It is not good either to indulge or suppress the desire. The best way is simply to watch the desire and see deeply into the nature of the desire, which is accompanied by suffering of its loss.

Such "seeing deeply into the nature of the desire" is not at all easy; it requires long training and continual practice. One of the strengths of the Theravada tradition—and of the Sayadaw's teachings—is the emphasis on individual practice. The Buddha himself worked hard for his liberation; among his last words were "Be a lamp unto yourselves. Work out your own salvation with diligence." Read Taungpulu's teachings and you too will be struck as I have been by his almost ruthless insistence that while *Nibbana* does exist and is ultimate reality, it is not given by a god or a guru, but has to be earned by utterly devoted practice of mindfulness in every dimension. As the Buddha said, "Non-greed is at the root of charity, non-hatred is at the root of morality, and non-delusion is at the root of mental development." For non-greed, non-hatred, and non-delusion to become natural and spontaneous, the whole personality has to be radically reorganized around a new center of awakened knowledge. These teachings explore that all-saving and all-purifying knowledge doggedly from every angle, and with an urgent simplicity that will inspire anyone, whatever spiritual path they are on.

As Taungpulu Sayadaw reminds us,

> While one is being mindful and observing precepts, one is protecting oneself, one does not harm oneself or another. In this way, the one who is being mindful with precepts also protects others.

Such words, and the example of the luminous and loving being who spoke and exemplified them, calmly challenge us to remember where our true responsibilities and joys lie.

Andrew Harvey
San Francisco, California
June 1996

Like a flame that has been blown out by a strong wind,
goes to rest and cannot be defined,
just so the sage who is freed from name and body,
goes to rest and cannot be defined.

Sutta Nipata, v. 1074

Gold From Gold

Anne Teich

⸰⸰⸰

Burma (Myanmar), the land once known as *Suvannabhumi*—the Golden Earth—received the teachings of Gotama Buddha well before the Christian era, but the recorded history of Buddhism in that country did not begin until the fifth century C.E. By the eleventh century, the Theravada (which lays claim to being the oldest school and which means "The Way of the Elders") had been firmly established over other forms of Buddhism and became the country's official religion under the patronage of kings. The vestiges of this period can still be seen and felt among the ruins of Pagan, the ancient capital, where 700 years ago patrons built thousands of religious monuments, as though in competition with one another, giving force and form to the glorious ascent of Burmese Buddhist culture.

The Buddha-Dhamma brought dignity, beauty, and sophistication to the daily life of the people. In a land blessed by abundant resources and warm-hearted people, Buddhism added what must be considered the noblest chapter in the country's history. Buddhist culture contributed to the spellbinding beauty and the dreamy, exotic mystique of "Golden Burma," as she was once called—timeless, beguiling, carefree—where, Kipling wrote, "the dawn comes up like thunder."

Great care and reverence toward the scriptures has always been the hallmark of monastic Buddhism in Burma, especially regarding the higher, philosophical teachings of the *Abhidhamma*. The *Abhidhamma* is the third of three collections of writings that make up the early Buddhist canon, the *Tipitaka* (Pali, literally: "three baskets." The *Vinaya-pitaka*, the first "basket," describes the monastic rules for monks and nuns; the *Sutta-pitaka*, the second, contains the discourses spoken by the Buddha to various groups). Monastery schools played an essential role in educating Burmese children in the Buddhist moral code which stresses generosity, nonviolence, and "mental culture," the practice of meditation.

Intensive meditation practice, which leads to the highest liberation known as *nibbana*—the legacy of the Buddhas—became eclipsed by centuries of monastic scholasticism and the merit-making activities of lay followers. The sacred words of the texts, preserved in monasteries and in human memory, were read at religious functions, but instruction in the practice of meditation, which could lead the practitioner to liberation in one lifetime, was not taken up in an earnest way. The German-born monk Nyanaponika (1901–1993), co-founder of the Buddhist Publication Society in Sri Lanka, has described the reemergence of meditation in Burmese Buddhism in his classic work *The Heart of Buddhist Meditation:*

> [T]he true understanding and the actual practice have been lagging far behind a mainly devotional attitude and an intellectual appreciation. It was in Burma, in this twentieth century, that a deep-reaching change was effected in that situation by monks who, by their searching spirit, clearly outlined again the singular features of the Way of Mindfulness....
>
> It was at the beginning of this century that a Burmese monk, U Narada by name, bent on actual realization of the teachings he had learnt, was eagerly searching for a system of meditation offering a direct access to the Highest Goal, without encumbrance by accessories. Wandering through the country, he met many who were given to strict meditative practice, but he could not obtain guidance satisfactory to him. In the course of his quest, coming to the famous meditation-caves in the hills of Sagaing in Upper

Burma, he met a monk who was reputed to have entered upon these lofty Paths of Sanctitude *(ariya-magga)* where the final achievement of Liberation is assured. When the Venerable U Narada put his question to him, he was asked in return: "Why are you searching outside of the Master's word? Has not the Only Way, Satipatthana, been proclaimed by Him?"

U Narada took up this indication. Studying again the text and its traditional exposition, reflecting deeply on it, and entering energetically upon its practice, he finally came to understand its salient features. The results achieved in his own practice convinced him that he had found what he was searching for: a clear-cut and effective method of training the mind for highest realization. From his own experience he developed the principles and the details of the practice which formed the basis for those who followed him as his direct or indirect disciples.

The pupils of the Venerable U Narada spread the knowledge of his method in Burma as well as in other Buddhist countries, and many were greatly benefited by it in their progress on the Path. The Venerable U Narada Mahathera, widely known in Burma as the Jetavan (or Mingun) Sayadaw, passed away on the 18th March 1955, aged 87. Many believe that he attained to final Deliverance *(Arahatta)*.[1]

In Theravada Buddhism, monastic seniority is calculated by the number of years a monk has been ordained, rather than by his chronological age. This simple arrangement prevents confusion and establishes an etiquette which is strictly observed, but it does not necessarily provide for nor ensure a succession of spiritually enlightened leaders. As with the waxing and waning of the Sasana Era itself (the time period in which the Buddha's teaching lives in the world), it is the understanding among Theravada Buddhists that enlightened teachers appear or do not appear with the changing fortunes of the times. When such masters do appear, it is said, they will be recognized by the people.

It was one such auspicious time when the cave-dwelling monk mentioned in Nyanaponika's account, called Potila Sayadaw, and his successors appeared. This heralded the revival of a long-dormant spiritual ideal: the perfection of virtue (the first step toward enlightenment) through *dhutanga* (ascetic) practices. For centuries the spiritual practice of *kudo*—salvation in the distant future through the practice of generosity and virtuous conduct in the present— had dominated popular religious practice. When *dhutanga* practice, the ancient "path of purification," reappeared, it was as though the fruit of a millennium of meritorious deeds had finally ripened.

There are few sights more formidable than a *dhutanga* monk. He lives alone for long periods of time in isolated forest settings, with the sole purpose of mastering his body and mind through meditation. A *dhutanga* monk will live outdoors with only three robes; he will go to the cemetery for meditation. He will struggle hard to overcome his loneliness and hunger, but the greatest part of his effort—like that of Gotama Buddha—will be directed toward conquering fear:

> I dwelt in such awe-inspiring abodes as orchard shrines, woodland shrines and tree shrines, which make the hair stand up. And while I dwelt there, a deer would approach me, or a peacock would knock off a branch, or the wind would rustle the leaves. Then I thought: Surely this is the fear and dread coming.
>
> I thought: Why do I dwell in constant expectation of the fear and dread? Why not subdue that fear and dread while maintaining the posture I am in when it comes to me?
>
> And while I walked, the fear and dread came upon me; but I neither stood nor sat nor lay down till I had subdued

that fear and dread. While I stood, the fear and dread came upon me; but I neither walked nor sat nor lay down till I had subdued that fear and dread. While I sat, the fear and dread came upon me; but I neither walked nor stood nor lay down till I had subdued that fear and dread. While I lay, the fear and dread came upon me; but I neither walked nor stood nor sat till I had subdued that fear and dread.[2]

If the monk's practice is good, harmful spirits may try to distract him and he will have to subdue them; and kindly spirits—even snakes—will protect him. As the result of his efforts, he may acquire supramundane abilities such as flying, knowing the thoughts of others, the power to heal, etc. Eventually, people will be attracted to him and request him to stay in their vicinity. The restrictive and highly regulated practices are intended to clear away the clutter of social and psychological life. Nothing should stand in the way of working towards refined states of meditation. *Dhutanga* practices are undertaken as a kind of spiritual athletic training and are considered (surprisingly) to be a "middle path" between extreme physical denial and physical overindulgence. The practices are an example of right effort. They presuppose that "The ideas of a man arise and disappear through a cause, through a condition. By means of training some ideas arise, by means of training other ideas disappear."[3]

During the period of strictest observance—sometimes lasting for decades—a *dhutanga* monk will follow as many as possible of these thirteen practices:

1. Wearing robes made of refuse materials.
2. Owning only three robes.
3. Eating only the food gathered from the alms-round.
4. Going from house to house for alms.
5. Eating in one session.

6. Using only one bowl for eating.
7. Refusing a second offering.
8. Dwelling in the forest.
9. Dwelling at the foot of a tree.
10. Dwelling in the open air.
11. Dwelling in a cemetery.
12. Accepting whatever resting place is given.
13. Never lying down.[4]

Dhutanga monks speak only to teach, look only to see where they are going, sleep only four hours a night, and eat only once a day and only what has been given to them in one bowl. They prefer living in remote areas where social contact is minimal. Their austere life is designed to promote contentment, humility, seclusion, and wakefulness. Living alone in deserted areas makes them fearless, simplicity makes them good-humored, an insecure existence makes them compassionate, the practice of mindfulness makes them energetic, and memorization and review of lengthy texts makes them knowledgable. Their appearance in a village elicits great respect and veneration among the people.

While they live as hermits, if they have cultivated compassion properly, *dhutanga* monks will seek to minister to others through teaching. This was the practice of the Very Venerable Taungpulu Sayadaw after he returned to society and until his death in June 1986. The ascetic practice of *dhutanga* monks is too rigorous for most people to follow, but the presence of such a monk is a living reminder of Buddha's achievement: *nibbana* and its singular goal of liberation from suffering. When you become ready to leave the great Round (*samsara*, the cycle of birth-and-rebirth for countless lifetimes), and when through your lifetimes of practice you have earned the laying-down of the burdens of the Round, *here* by these practices you will find the door.

A Brief Biography

Who was the Very Venerable Taungpulu Tawya Kaba-Aye Sayadaw Phaya? Much is revealed in the meaning of his name:

Taungpulu means "haunted hill." He chose to practice in such a place because it was lonely, even forbidding.

Tawya means "forest." Sayadaw was a forest-dwelling monk who observed the thirteen ascetic practices taught by the Buddha.

Kaba-Aye means "world peace." This was the title conferred on him by the Sixth Buddhist Council held in Rangoon, Burma in 1956.

Sayadaw means "senior monk," one who has been a monk for twenty years or more and is a teacher.

Phaya means "lord" or "reverend one."

In 1978, at the age of eighty, Taungpulu Sayadaw left his homeland for the first time and traveled to the United States four times at the invitation of his senior student, Dr. Rina Sircar, professor of Buddhist Studies at the California Institute of Integral Studies in San Francisco. During these visits, he gave discourses, performed ordinations, established a forest monastery, the Taungpulu Kaba-Aye Monastery in Boulder Creek, California, and oversaw the building of the Shwe Thein Daw World Peace Pagoda, the first pagoda in the Burmese style constructed in North America. In 1990, a relic from his body was enshrined in the Kaba-Thukha Aye Zedi memorial stupa at the Boulder Creek monastery.

I have chosen the word *wildflower* to describe Taungpulu Sayadaw because the wildflower is one of nature's humblest and most adorned creations, the supreme example of the divine at play, creating beauty for its own sake. Through great effort, and with only a few weeks to live, wildflowers bloom in rocky crags, on riverbanks, and in meadows. They often live out their brief but vibrant lives hidden from anyone's eyes in shimmering silence, a splash of brillaint color on nature's canvas.

Taungpulu Sayadaw was just like a wildflower, living a hidden, solitary life for many years in pursuit of spiritual achievement. He knew that the sainthood of the Buddhas and Bodhisattvas of the past still exists and is worthy to be emulated. He would have practiced this way contentedly for the rest of his life were it not for the public recognition of his spiritual accomplishment. Albert Sircar, M.D., Rina's brother, an army doctor stationed in the area where Taungpulu lived, had been called once to attend the Sayadaw when he was very ill. When Dr. Sircar attempted to give him an injection, the Sayadaw pointed to a plant in the room and told him to give the medicine to the plant. The Sayadaw recovered, and Rina's brother invited him to visit his family in Rangoon. This was the beginning of a thirty-year friendship between Taungpulu Sayadaw and the Sircar family, and a ministry which took the wildflower monk around the world.

Though born into village life, Taungpulu Sayadaw came from royal lineage; he is the descendant of King Anawratha and King Kya Swa. There is not yet a published biography giving a full account of the Sayadaw's life, and it is my earnest hope that one day the complete story will be told. The following excerpt from an anonymous devotee's comprehensive obituary in *The Working People's Daily* (published in Rangoon, Wednesday, June 25, 1986) recounts highlights of Taungpulu Sayadaw's life:

> When a man of might and magnitude, especially one who is held in immense affection and esteem by his dependents or followers, passes away, the usual saying in Burmese is "The Great Golden Mountain has dropped and fallen!" Now we have to say exactly the same with deep sorrow, for the Taungpulu Kaba-Aye Sayadaw has very recently expired. To be precise, the sad event took place at 8:04 a.m. on Saturday,

Who dare blame him who is like refined gold?
Even Devas praise him; by Brahma too he is
praised. (Verse 230)

the 15th waning day of Kason, 1348 B.E. (7-6-86) at the
Taungpulu Sutaungpyi Kyaung Taik, 70 University Avenue,
Rangoon. The Sayadaw's age was 90.

The Sayadaw was born of U Yan and Daw Shwe The on
Saturday, the third waning day of Tabaung, 1258 B.E., at
Tezu, a big village in the Township of Wundwin, Mandalay
Division. His name was Maung Paw Lar. When Maung Paw
Lar was seven years old his peasant parents entrusted him
for education to the Sayadaw of the Yewun Monastery of

the village. He was taught the rudiments of reading and writing Burmese and Pali. U Lakkhana, a resident monk of the monastery, was responsible for his knowledge of Pali grammar and Thingyo, the fundamentals of the Abhidhamma.

At the age of fourteen Maung Paw Lar was ordained a novice by U Teja with his parents as "donors." (A donor of an ordination is one who sponsors the occasion by supplying the requisites and bearing the expenses, if any.) He was then named Shin Nandiya. Seven years after his novitiation, Shin Nandiya received higher ordination from his precetor U Teja, his donors this time being U Tun Aye and Daw Kyar Hmway. Shin Nandiya thus became U Nandiya.

U Nandiya studied under his preceptor U Teja while serving him for four years. In his fifth year he went to Mandalay for further studies. Staying at the Shwebo Monastery of the Dakkhinarama Payagyi Taik he studied the Abhidhamma proper at the feet of U Acara of the monastery. His teacher of the Vinaya was U Narada. His other Mandalay teachers of repute included U Neyya and U Tejavamsa who taught him certain commentaries on the Vinaya. To extend the horizon of his knowledge he approached U Sasana of Pakokku school of learning under whom he read the Vinaya once again and all three volumes of the Suttanta Pitaka. Thus his knowledge of the Three Canons was rounded off and he became well-versed in both Mandalay and Pakokku traditions of scriptural education.

U Nandiya's career began with dissemination of knowledge in the literary field. He started teaching a host of pupils numbering more than a hundred at the Yelai Monastery of Thazi which he accepted at the request of U Nandobhasa.

He remained there shouldering the teaching responsibilities until his twentieth year of standing as a monk.

The Sayadaw U Nandiya's real desire had all along been to practice the Dhamma. He saw *Pariyatti* or Learning only as a stepping-stone to *Patipatti* or Practice. Now he considered himself to have been fully equipped with theoretical knowledge to proceed to the practicing stage which was far more important. Accordingly he renounced the monastery at Thazi. Turning his back to all his pupils he went to Thaton where the then famous Mingun Zetawun Sayadaw had founded a meditation centre. He learned the Mingun Sayadaw's method of meditation and stayed there for two years. Another two years he spent at the village of Dhaywin six miles from Moulmein to take charge of meditation training there as he was urged by his teacher the Mingun Sayadaw.

The following twelve years saw U Nandiya's independent practice of the Dhamma in the environs of his native village Tezu. The Dhamma he practiced was twofold: vipassana meditation and dhutanga practices. He shunned people except on alms-rounds. From one secluded spot to another he moved devoting full time to the practical Dhamma. He was sometimes at Kyauksin, sometimes at Thayetchaung, and at other times at a place called Taungpulu near Meiktila. At that time a dam was being built at Taungpulu where his alms-round took him on certain days. Those who offered alms-food were then dam labourers. More often than not he made make-shift residence at the foot of a tree, near a bush or close to a boulder. He was, however, never seen lying on his back, one of the dhutanga practices that he kept till his demise. His ascetic practices were so severe that some speech organ in his throat was impaired for life, and he could speak only in a very low voice.

One day the officials of the dam construction who had been watching and were struck with awe by his rigorous asceticism, built a small bamboo hut and offered it to him. The hut formed the seed which in due course developed into the present estate of buildings including a few brick ones. The Taungpulu Monastery, a haven to all who came to seek peace of mind, was born!

Since then U Nandiya has come to be known far and wide as Taungpulu Sayadaw. His laying of the foundation stone of the Kaba-Aye Pagoda built by the officials and labourers probably to mark the completion of the dam construction on the nearby hillock earned him the extended appellation—Taungpulu Kaba-Aye Sayadaw.

The devotion to the Sayadaw by his followers was testified to by their participation in the building of the Myanyinzu Pagoda at Tezu under the Sayadaw's auspices and also by their ordinations for short stays with the Sayadaw as their preceptor. As regards the former, the original pagoda under the same name was historical but had long been in ruin. It was therefore the Sayadaw's idea to construct a new one covering the old and on the model of the great Shwedagon of Rangoon. The construction was started in October 1975, and it took two years and eight months to complete it. The height of the pagoa is 111 cubits, one htwar, one mite, one inch and one finger equivalent to about 166 feet. The Burmese measurement having seven figures all being one, symbolizes the seven Factors of Enlightenment. People made donations not only of money but also of jewelry and gems for enshrinement together with religious objects. What was more significant was voluntary labor contributed by more than fifty thousand people representing various nationalities of the Union.

In the footsteps of the Buddha and Mahatheras of old, the Sayadaw travelled all over the country on missionary tours. From Myitkyina to Mergui, from Sittwe to Keng Tung, there was scarcely any place any place that the Sayadaw had not set foot on. At the invitation of local devotees the Sayadaw visited and wherever he did there was welcome, most cordial and gratifying. His metta or loving kindness was responded to with the heartiest and humblest homage paid by the devotees.

~

In 1954, when U Nandiya (Taungpulu Sayadaw's name as a junior monk) heard that his teacher Jetavana Mingon Sayadaw had died, he walked many miles to pay his last respects to the body, which was guarded by a snake. It is said that only upon the arrival of U Nandiya did the snake depart. Like his teacher, and his teacher's teacher, U Nandiya had spent years living and practicing in caves or in the open, alone, without speaking. Even when he sometimes became weak or ill, he refused to lessen his effort.

It has been said that during a period of complete dedication to the *dhutanga* practice, U Nandiya would rest while standing and holding onto a rope tied to a tree. His diligence brought him renown and drew many people who wished to pay their respects. It became increasingly difficult for him to practice without interruption, so he made the decision to leave the area where he was then staying to go to an even more remote and secluded forest. One night as he was preparing to leave, a beautiful *deva* (a being who lives in a heavenly plane) appeared and pleaded with him to stay. He replied, "One day I will return, but for now I am moving to Tha Bye Chang forest."

The years spent on the arid plains of central Burma, where summer temperatures rise to 105 degrees, did not leave the Sayadaw austere or aloof. When I first met the eighty-year-old monk in

1977, he was fully relaxed and acutely alert; he spoke only when he had something meaningful to relate, and smiled and laughed freely. Taungpulu Sayadaw was always willing to teach his audience, day or night, and he taught according to the oral tradition of his ancestors—through stories, recitation, and repetition of chants and prayers. Just seeing him was a powerful teaching in the spiritual benefits of living a simple, strenuous life of renunciation.

The Significance of Taungpulu Sayadaw and His Teachings

The time has passed for seeing and hearing this master teacher, but Taungpulu lives on in memory. What will the people who knew him remember best of his many wonderful qualities? His bearing, his kindness, his smile—called *hasituppada*, the smile of the *arahat*—his patience, the sound of his voice, his creative way of teaching, the miracles attributed to him, his complete freedom within a daily routine of great physical discipline, his love of nature? During his lifetime he was referred to as "the one complete in the three *sikhas*" (virtues, concentration, wisdom).

Within the austere routine of his daily life, and in his one-pointed effort to teach the importance of practicing mindfulness meditation, the Sayadaw transcended tradition and place. The broadminded and kindly nature for which he was beloved by all was beyond doctrine and culture. The years of attentive meditation stripped away conventional social and psychological limits, leaving the Sayadaw with a boundary-less quality. He lived in a state of freedom which often gave his face a look of surprise, as though he was encountering the world for the first time. The Sayadaw never referred to himself in the first person; he was always *pongyi*—"this monk."

Taungpulu Sayadaw's teaching was rooted in the scriptures of the Theravada tradition and the triadic discipline of philosophy,

psychology, and ethics. The salient points of these three inter-
woven paths is summed up in this verse from the *Dhammapada:*

Not to do any evil,
To cultivate good,
To purify one's mind,
This is the advice of the Buddhas.[5]

Taungpulu Sayadaw often illustrated his simple, clear presen-
tation of complex topics with rhymes, stories, and laughter. But
the moral of every lesson was always the same: meditate and you
will *see* the world in that extraordinary way which awakens the
mind.

The Sayadaw taught that each station in life holds the possibility for high spiritual attainment; he did not preach that everyone should become monks and nuns and undertake ascetic practices
in order to attain *arahat*ship and enter *nibbana.* Of greater signif-
icance to him was one's *approach* to meditation, the attitude with
which to take up the practice. Within the pendulum movement
of concentrated attention and flexibility, of striving and patience,
lies the key to progress.

Strive but do not strain: "If you sit until you have too much
pain, you will lose your concentration, you will get angry, and
you won't be able to meditate," he would say. Move your position, but move with mindfulness. Everyone can practice mindfulness, no matter who they are or where and how they live, because
mindfulness is a mental quality brought to bear on the activities of
one's mind and body. It is not a lifestyle or a philosophy—it is a
practice. Know when you have reached a limit. Do not overextend
yourself so that you become too tired, too discouraged, too weak
to continue. You will not make progress in this way. If you are a
layperson and you live with faith and observe the Five Precepts
you can attain much, even the first stage of sainthood! Why did

the Sayadaw always emphasize the ideal of *sotapanna* (the first stage of sainthood, with only seven more lives remaining) rather than that of the *arahat?* Reducing an infinite number of lifetimes to seven lifetimes, he said, is a much harder accomplishment than reducing seven lifetimes to a last rebirth.

He often advised practitioners to take up the Eight or Ten Precepts from time to time, and to take up ordination for awhile. These periods of focused practice have immense benefit. In quiet surroundings away from distractions you can calm yourself and see things differently. Hardly anyone wants to live in a monastery for life, but even the layperson who keeps precepts and practices meditation is a kind of *bhikkhu* (monk), he said, for in one way *bhikkhu* means destroying the defilements (such as greed, hatred, and delusion) which keep us in a state of suffering.

What took place during his long years of solitary practice can only be known by the few who have attempted it, but the results were visible to everyone who ever met Taungpulu Sayadaw. His life will be remembered as an extraordinary event that confirmed the written word of the Buddha-Dhamma through its living example.

A Great Alchemy

With the *arahat* ideal of Theravada Buddhism, the pathway to enlightenment of the early *Sangha* (the community of monks) took on a transcendent character that turned its back on the world and tried to escape suffering rather than alleviating it. At worst, monasticism was a selfish, life-denying response to the problems of existence. The Gotama Buddha of the early scriptures taught that cessation of suffering was possible, and to this end he promulgated the *satipatthana-vipassana* (mindfulness and insight) method of meditation as the only way "for the purification of beings, for the overcoming of sorrow and lamentation, for the destruction of suffering and grief, for reaching the right path, for the attain-

ment of *Nibbana.*⁶ The Buddha was responding, both as reformer
and revolutionary, to the spiritual and philosophical deadend of
Indian society created by the caste system, speculative philosophies,
and a corrupt priesthood. By elevating personal effort and equal-
ity, Gotoma's creed answered confusion and doubt, but his teachings could not resolve the dualism created by a fatalistic worldview:
life is a curse which must be lifted. The dilemma of *samsara* vs. *nibbana* has remained.

Soon after the Buddha's death *(parinibbana)* in approximately
544 B.C.E., the followers of the Buddha divided themselves into
two schools of thought. The teachings and sayings of the Buddha
were collectively accepted and committed to group memory in the
years immediately following the *parinibbana*, and were preserved
in oral transmission for the next 200 years. Succeeding generations
of monks who recited and eventually recorded them claimed that
this body of teaching represented the totality of what the Buddha
had taught. In these scriptures, the Buddha teaches *nibbana* as
the supreme spiritual attainment: this state should be sought above
all others, and if possible achieved in this life. In this way, the ideal
of the *arahat* became identified as the only goal worth pursuing by
the monastic *Sangha*, while the laity gradually became excluded
from the possibility of significant spiritual progress.

As other schools of thought rose to prominence, scriptures of
a different nature began to appear, forming the basis of what came
to be called Mahayana ("Great Vehicle") Buddhism. Mahayana followers developed the ideal of the *bodhisattva*, a spiritually realized being who forfeits his or her personal liberation in order to
lead an infinite number of beings onto the path of enlightenment.

The two ideals have been carried forward by diverse cultures
through the succeeding two-and-a-half millennia. There has never
been any likelihood that the two schools would ever meet and amal-
gamate. The zealous guardians of the Theravada *Tipitaka* preserved

the early teachings in a kind of time capsule—the island of Sri Lanka—for centuries. Later schools continued "finding" new sutras and produced a vast body of literature, which they in turn claimed to be what the Buddha *really* taught.

Taungpulu Sayadaw's spiritual attainment seemed to be a convergence of these two ideals. After his death, two opinions emerged regarding the Sayadaw's identity and his destiny: many asserted that he had passed away, like his teacher, as an *arahat*; for he had said many times over the years:

> Why do you love flowers? Are they doing anything for you? Do they help you cook and clean? Can they bring you water? Yet you offer flowers to the shrine; with flowers you cheer up a sick person, or decorate a dark corner of the house.
>
> So it is with the *arahat*. Like a flower, the *arahat* is beautiful to see and has a sweet fragrance. Like a flower, the *arahat* brings joy and tranquility to the mind.

Few are there amongst men who go Beyond.... (Verse 85)
Just before Taungpulu Sayadaw's cremation, a news reporter from Bangkok took a picture of his body in the glass coffin. When the film was developed, the image revealed Sayadaw's upraised hand in what many feel is a gesture of blessing.

You have to go to the flower to enjoy its beauty; it is
the same with the *arahat*, for he will never come to you.

Nevertheless, others maintained confidently, basing their claims
on eyewitness reports,[7] that Sayadaw was a *phaya-supan*—a future
Buddha, whose life in this century was just one of countless lifetimes spent progressing toward Buddhahood. In a staunch
Theravada culture, how could this be a viable possibility?

The *bodhisattva*'s career is discussed in several places in the Pali
Canon: the *Nidana Katha*, the *Jatakamala*, and the *Buddhavamsa*.
In the *Nidana Katha (The Story of the Lineage)*, Sumedho, a powerful sage on the verge of enlightenment, encounters a Buddha and
the attending crowds who are greatly benfited by such a being's
presence; on seeing this, Sumedho proclaims a desire to follow
in the Buddha's footsteps. His eye of compassion now opened,
the sage receives a blessing from the Buddha and goes in search
of the qualities which are necessary to qualify him as a Buddha.
This vow leads him to life-after-life struggles to perfect the *paramis*—
psychological qualities which represent extraordinary spiritual
achievement: generosity, virtue, renunciation, energy, patience,
truthfulness, determination, loving-kindness, equanimity, and wisdom—and culminates with a last lifetime as a Buddha in some
future eon. There exists in the Theravada Buddhist canon, then,
both the ideal of the *arahat*—praised by the Buddha as the enlightened being who has vanquished the enemies of greed, hatred,
and delusion, representative of a spiritual stage worth striving
for; and the *bodhisattva*, who through his compassion for others
takes up a further stage of spiritual commitment.

It is easy to see the best of both worlds in the personality of
Taungpulu Sayadaw. Those who knew him can testify to Taungpulu's
one-pointed effort, his dedication to tireless practice, his gaze, and
the no-nonsense approach. But there was also a profound *spa-
ciousness*, an expanded—indeed, illimitable—human heart in a state

of quiet exhaltation. The extraordinary balance of this *maha-purisa* (great being) offers the two ideals an *entente cordiale*.

In our age there are very few wildflower saints. When such a person reaches an enlightened state, they are not attached to the body, so the people around them must request them to stay on. Such saints reside in supramundane states of mind, completely unaffected by discursive thoughts and concerns. Though they still have a foothold in the physical world, they live in a way which appears to us strange, mysterious, and eccentric. These great beings see differently, speak differently, eat differently, behave differently. They eat less, their rhythms of rest and activity are different, and they seem to exude a fragrance of sanctity. In their presence, you feel peaceful, as though you are sitting next to a clear, still pool on a summer day. Your personal concerns are replaced by an overwhelming sense of relief and equanimity.

Taungpulu Sayadaw had fully developed the all-knowing mind, the mind which has the power of infinite range. He was known to heal simply by giving a small glass of blessed water, or even by a glance. People reported being protected by him in life-threatening situations. He would give you advice if you asked, but mostly he remained silent. Outwardly his life appeared monotonous, yet miraculous incidents surrounded him. He was seen walking on water, flying through the air; he released the dead from the in-between states, snakes protected him, animals of all kinds would greet him when he appeared, and even deer came out of the forest to pay their respects.

Miraculous powers are such a novel experience for Westerners raised in a culture which praises rationality that we easily become attracted to and even mesmerized by them. If we are unschooled in the psychology of sainthood, we may think that miraculous powers equal spiritual attainment. This is not the case, however. Those with "miraculous" powers may lack the altruistic intention of helping others; they may be intoxicated with their own powers. Only a true saint embodies humility, compassion, and skilfull means while using his or her powers to help others.

It is a spiritual boon to meet such a person. But even if we have had the good fortune to encounter a saint, this is not enough. We must at some point take up the task of transformation ourselves, with our own effort. For this reason *energy* is one of the requisites of the enlightened mind.

↝

The teachings and practices of Buddhism are taking strong root in the West. As practitioners, we seek expressions appropriate for our time while struggling to protect the essence of teachings and traditions that are thousands of years old. Such concerns are not necessarily shared by the messengers who offer us the teachings.

The Venerable Taungpulu Sayadaw encouraged the establishment of a monastic *sangha* in America; he especially emphasized the quality of patience necessary to bring it about. As the Sayadaw said during his last visit to the United States:

> The *sasana* is only in its beginning stages here in America. Only if there are at least five monks here will it be possible to conduct ordinations. If it is not possible to ordain new monks, the *sasana* will not have a chance to grow. Therefore, please be patient and try to support the monks who are staying here.
>
> In order for the *sasana* to be established in America, the Americans who have the desire to become monks should do so. They should study and practice the Dhamma so that they can later teach others. Thus will the continuity of the *sasana* be established.
>
> The monks from Burma will be staying here only a short while. Most of the Burmese monks don't want to stay in America. They will eventually go back. Therefore, in the long run, those Americans who become monks will carry on

the *sasana*. They are the only ones who can really establish the *sasana* in this country. People from the outside, from far away, cannot really do much.

Therefore the lay-community should support these American monks with the proper requisites and should encourage them to stay here. You should encourage them to study and to practice the Dhamma, and later on to teach the Dhamma. Then only will America be like Burma some day, with many monasteries where even little children can come to study and learn about the Buddha's teachings.[8]

Taungpulu Sayadaw emphasized and exemplified the benefits of monastic life, encouraging even short-term ordination as an avenue of spiritual benefit. But he also encouraged householders to observe the Five Precepts as a path of spiritual initiation and as an act of great charity. His creative and sympathetic personality endeared him to every person he met, regardless of their ethnicity, gender, age, or culture. He trusted, respected, and relied upon women, and elevated their status as much as possible within a religious hierarchy dominated by men. He encouraged Rina to pursue higher education, nicknaming her "College," and made sure she took the exams along with the monks. When Rina worked to establish the monastery in Boulder Creek, Sayadaw changed her nickname to "Visakha"—chief benefactoress of the Buddha and his *Sangha*. Rina traveled with Sayadaw as his translator, and helped him lead retreats. He would instruct the monks to sit with her, thus making a clear statement that women have an equal place in the teaching of Dhamma.

Regarding spiritual qualities, Taungpulu Sayadaw believed that patience is the noblest attitude, and that there is no practice more excellent than the perfection of patience. Without it, there can be no prosperity, no growth, and no positive development.

The mindful exert themselves; to no abode are they attached. Like swans that quit their pools, home after home they abandon. (Verse 91) Taungpulu Sayadaw and Rina Sircar in Burma, 1977.

The teachings given by Taungpulu Sayadaw in this book are not new; all can be found in the Pali Canon. But they reflect his straightforward way: practice mindfulness and clear comprehension. In every situation, he often said, there is an opportunity to practice. Even if only for the duration of ten snappings of the fingers, practice mindfulness.

Spiritual practice strengthens the powers of higher understanding and contributes to the well-being of a culture. From the Buddhist perspective, this higher understanding is possible through the experience of *vipassana:* the most discriminating kind of seeing. The Venerable Taungpulu Sayadaw taught the mindfulness method of meditation in conjunction with observance of the Five Precepts as a means of achieving *vipassana.* The precepts purify and protect the mind and body, promoting receptivity so that calm, con-

centration, and mindfulness can arise. The cognitive exercises which
are a salient feature of early Buddhist psychology increase insight-
knowledge, a "seeing" which has transformative power. Insight-
knowledge leads to acceptance, the fundamental component for
healing of any kind, and which is in itself a prerequisite for the
experience of true freedom.

The teachings collected in this book reflect the qualities of
someone who had achieved both healing and freedom; they are his
declarations because Taungpulu Sayadaw never wrote anything
for publication. They represent a popular sample—by no means
a comprehensive collection—transcribed from taped discourses
and collected from talks given by Taungpulu Sayadaw during his
visits to the United States. "The Efficacy of Sarana-Gamana"
and "Maha Satipatthana Vipassana—Insight Meditation" are reprint-
ed with permission from the Religious Ministry of Burma.

This book has been compiled in honor of Taungpulu Sayadaw's
life and work on behalf of the Sasana Era, and in respectful memory of the tenth year of his passing.

May all beings be happy.
May all beings be peaceful.
May all beings be liberated.

[1] Nyanaponika Thera, *The Heart of Buddhist Meditation* (New York: Samuel Weiser, Inc., 1962), pp. 85–86.

[2] Bhikkhu Nanamoli, *The Life of the Buddha* (Kandy, Sri Lanka: Buddhist Publication Society, 1978), pp. 15–16.

[3] Rune E. A. Johnansson, *Pali Buddhist Texts Expained to the Beginner* (Stockholm, Sweden: Scandinavian Institute of Asian Studies, Monograph Series No. 14, 1973), p. 52.

[4] Bhadantacariya Buddhaghosa, *The Path of Purification*, (Kandy, Sri Lanka: Buddhist Publication Society, 1975), p. 59.

[5] Narada Maha Thera, translator, *The Dhammapada* (Calcutta: Maha Bodhi Society of India, 1962), p. 133.

[6] Soma Thera, translator, *The Way of Mindfulness* (Kandy, Sri Lanka: Buddhist Publication Society, 1981), p. 1.

[7] The late Venerable Mahasi Sayadaw and Taungpulu Sayadaw were both students of Jetavana Mingon Sayadaw. According to Mahasi Sayadaw, Jetavana Mingon Sayadaw asked one of his students to take up the *bodhisattva* path, and that it was Taungpulu Sayadaw who had done so. In a separate report, one of Taungpulu Sayadaw's disciples said that the Sayadaw had once pointed out on a map of India the locale where he would be reborn in a future time.

[8] *Forest Light News*, Vol. 2, 1984, pp. 1–2.

The Teachings

Three Times Knowing

August 16, 1978
Translated by Rina Sircar

Thweti
Wen ti—
Tonje hi
Thi yin bhawana.
ॐ

Here is a meditation technique:

Breathing in, touching
Breathing out, touching
Bring your mind to the touching
So, three times knowing, you have a meditation.

Here is how it relates to dependent origination: If we know, then we will break away from the vicious circle of *samsara*. If we are under the spell of ignorance, then we have to go and come back, go and come back. Dependent origination means one thing is depending on the other, and so everything is always changing. When one thing is arising, another thing is ceasing. Arising, ceasing, arising, ceasing. So when you breathe in, it follows that you must breathe out. Bring your awareness to this process; you will gain knowledge with every breath. Once again, here is the verse for dependent origination:

Mati awessa, thi wesa
Napya que we ma
Mati lim pa, ti lim pya
Patessa tomopa.

If you know, there is no more ignorance. If you do not know, it is ignorance, and you go around and around; you will have to come back. If you know, there is knowledge and cessation. This is dependent origination.

The Car and the Driver

August 6, 1978
Translated by Rina Sircar

೨೧

The body and mind are like the car and its driver. Whenever the driver will start the car, only then will the car go. The car cannot do anything without the driver. So we can say that the car is like the body, *rupa*, and driver is like the mind, *nama*.

Only when matter makes contact with mind, then you can know this is this, and that is that.

Concept and Reality

June 26, 1983

Translated by Rina Sircar

ᴣ

Today the discourse will be on concept and reality and Sayadaw will explain these two and the differences between them.

Repeat the phrase "*Seik, seikdete, yoke, naibban—paramata taya lebah.*"

The phrase means "Consciousness, mental factors, materiality, and *nibbana*—these are the four ultimate realities." Why are they called the "ultimate realities?" We can experience these realities in our day-to-day life, and that is why they are called the ultimate realities. There are four ultimate realities: *seik*, which is mind; *seikdete*, which is mental factors; *yo*, which is matter; and *naibban*, which is *nibbana*. These are the four ultimate realities.

These four can be categorized in another way. Mind and mental factors come under one category called *na* or *nama*, or the knowing faculty. *Yo* is materiality. Accordingly, the living beings in the thirty-one planes of existence* are all *na-yo*. They have a mind and they have a body; they are mentality and materiality.

Also, *yo* can be analyzed further. There are four primary elements. The four are: *pathavi*, the earth or solidity; *apo*, which means liquidity or water; *tejo*, or temperature, either heat or cold; and *vayo*, which means the wind, or motion. These are the four primary elements. They will be followed by the four secondary elements, and they are *vanna*, which means shape; *gandha*, which is

---

* According to the teachings of the Buddha, there are thirty-one planes of existence to which we can be reborn according to our *kamma* accumulated in each life: four hell realms, the realm of human existence, six celestial realms inhabited by gods, sixteen pure abode realms of absorbed consciousness, and four formless realms.

smell; *yata*, which is taste; and *oja*, which means nutriment. These are the four secondary elements. In every matter you will have these eight elements—the four primary *(mahabhu)* and the four secondary; always these are together.

Now, out of the four ultimate realities, the three—that is mind, mental factors, and matter—are always destructible, they are vanishing all the time, but *nibbana* will never vanish. The first three ultimate realities are conditioned; therefore, they will arise and pass away. The fourth, ultimate reality—*nibbana*—is unconditioned, and it is such a thing that it will always be there.

All the living beings in the thirty-one planes of existence are *nama-rupa*, or mentality and materiality; they are conditioned because they arise and vanish, moment by moment and life by life. By means of language in order to communicate with one another, we describe the ulitmate conditioned reality by different names such as "I," "mine," "woman," "man," but when you look at all the living beings, they are ultimately all *na-yo*, they are mentality-materiality.

What and why are the ultimate realities? First of all, there are the Five Khandhas. An individual is viewed as a totality of five aggregates, and they are the ultimate realities, and they are real. So also, the twelve bases—*ayatana*. The eye, nose, ear, tongue, body, and mind are the six sense organs and every sense organ has its sense objects. Therefore, this becomes twelve and is called the Twelve Ayatanas which are also *parama* (ultimate) because we can experience them and can directly know them. There are eighteen elements which are also *parama*. And, also the Four Noble Truths are *parama*. These are all ultimate realities, but just for the sake of simplicity they are also called the *na-yo*.

To experience the mentality and the materiality, that is, *na-yo*, which is the ultimate reality, one will have to practice and work hard.

Now here is a question to be answered: What do you call all these people? "Beings," we say. When you see a dog, you give a name. The suggestion is that instead of seeing the ultimate reality, *na-yo*, which has mind and body, we at once give a name, "dog," and we make it a totally different thing, and we don't see the reality in the dog; we just call it a "dog," which is a concept. When we see the animal which is nothing but mentality and materiality, mind and body, we at once give a name—"That's a pig," we say, for example, and we take the pig as the reality, and we don't see the reality which is not the pig, but mind and matter.

Another example is a hen. When you see a hen, you call it "hen," but you don't see the *parama*, the ultimate reality; that hen is nothing but mind and body. Instead we at once give a name and try to categorize by giving it a name.

Whenever we see an animal, a goat, for example, it is not the reality we see, it is the concept, just the name. We categorize that animal as "goat," and we are missing the reality there, which is *na-yo*, or mind-matter, or mentality-materiality. Until we see that reality, the *na-yo*, it is very difficult to attain our goal. So all of us, to attain our goal, have to work hard and practice to reach that goal, to experience the *na-yo*, mentality-materiality.

When we see an animal, we say, "This is a cow," but "cow" is just *pinnya*, just concept. The reality of that animal is mind and matter. We do not see the reality, we at once give a name and put that animal in the world of concept, and call it "cow." We are missing the reality there: that animal is nothing but mind-matter, or mentality-materiality, or *nama-rupa*, or *na-yo*.

We do not try see the world of reality, we always try to live in the world of concept. We do not live in the real world, and whenever we see and man and a woman, we try to discriminate and give a name like "man" or "woman." We don't see them in their reality—which is mentality and materiality. Instead, we at once try

Whether in village or in forest, in vale or on hill, wherever Arahants dwell, delightful, indeed, is that spot. (Verse 98)

to give them a name and put them in the conceptual world, and miss the real mentality and materiality.

Now, about the non-living things which do not have mind, for example, tree, river, mountain, rock, gemstone. These are things which are only matter and do not have a mind.

Here is a question to be answered: With regard to reality and concept, which one lasts and which one dies?

What about the reality of John Kennedy? Which one is lasting, the reality or the concept "Kennedy"?

The name "Kennedy"—the concept is still there, it is lasting. His name is still there, but his reality, the mind-body, is it still there? No. So, the concept "Kennedy" is still there. Because the name "Kennedy" is still there, so you can say "Kennedy," but his mentality and materiality, the two ultimate realities, the mind and matter, are not there. The ultimate reality is gone, but the name and concept "Kennedy" is still there.

Which one do you all see? Do you see the concept or the reality? We see the concept. Do you see "Kennedy," which is concept? The concept is still there, but the reality—Kennedy's body and mind—is not there. The names are always there, even though they are not the real thing. But the real thing, which is the *parama*, is not there.

If you are looking for something, and then reach for it, what will you see, the reality or the concept? Suppose you pick up that object, what will you pick up, the reality or the concept? You will pick up the reality. If you touch it with your finger and you feel it, what do you feel? The ultimate reality or the concept? The *parama*.

Now, two persons are standing: one is a woman and the other is a man. With your hand, can you feel the woman, and say this is woman? Or this is man? Can you differentiate the man and the woman? Yes. How do you discriminate? You have to feel the whole thing.

So, you cannot touch the concept, you can only feel and touch the reality. "Man" and "woman," the name, the concept, cannot be touched, cannot be felt. But the reality can be known—that they are mentality and materiality.

You can only touch the reality, the matter, and not the concept. You can't touch a man and you can't touch a woman, these are the concepts, but you can touch the reality.

We cannot touch just names and concepts, but we can touch the reality of the man and the reality of the woman. But we cannot touch a name or a concept.

What about a lime and a lemon? The taste of lime and lemon, is it sour? Lime is sour and lemon is sour. So, lime and lemon, is it reality or concept? It is concept. If the taste of lemon and lime is sour, so you can also taste the name "Kennedy," and lick and find out the taste of Kennedy, whether it is sweet or sour. Can you do that? No. So lime and lemon are just names. Of the four secondary realities, taste is one of them, and that is real. We give the name as "lime" and "lemon," but the taste sour is real.

Concept has no taste. The taste that we get, the sour taste, the sweet, the bitter—all those tastes, whatever taste we get, is the ultimate reality. All those names that we give like "lime" and "lemon," these are the names which we give out of habit. But the ultimate reality is the taste (a secondary quality).

Now chili pepper, is it hot or bitter? Hot. That chili pepper, is it reality or concept? So, chili pepper cannot be hot, but the taste is hot. What about salt? Do you get a salty taste from salt? Is salt reality or concept? The taste is real; saltiness is concept. Salt is the concept; but the salty taste is reality.

Whenever you talk about concept and reality, in the concept you will not find any taste. Taste, when you talk of it, is one of the secondary elements, and taste is then one of the ultimate realities. What are we seeing now, concept or reality? If we see shape and color, this is ultimate reality. So the name "Kennedy," which you all have said is concept, can you see that concept Kennedy? No. Concept cannot be seen, cannot be touched, cannot be felt. Only when it is reality can we then touch, feel, and see.

Only the ultimate reality exists, but we always see the concept. Because we have a wrong view of personal identity. This leads us to see the concept. In our day-to-day life, we live in the conceptual world, because to communicate we need language. Our habit is to categorize and when we see certain things as a certain shape and color we give that a name, so in our day-to-day life and for the sake of communication we live in the world of concept. We can't go and call each person "mentality and materiality." It would be very difficult to differentiate between people. It is for the sake of communication that we use all these concepts; otherwise it would be difficult. We use concept, which we come to depend on; then we lose sight of ultimate reality.

Now you see an image, you see only the image, but you are not differentiating man and woman. If you see the image of a man, or if you see the image of a woman, then you see the concept. But if you just see the image, not labeling it, then that it is *parama*, that is ultimate.

In our everyday life we have to use this conceptual language because we cannot separate ourselves from concept until we experience the ultimate reality of mentality and materiality. Then, of course, you will even stop talking. You have to practice a lot to get the experience of mentality and materiality. When you get the experience, when you will know for yourself, "This is mentality, this is materiality," then you will not use language that much. But until you get this experience yourself, as long as you don't see, and don't get to that stage, you will be using conceptual language.

This conventional language will be there, and all of us are using this concept for the sake of convenience. It is very convenient to use this conceptual language, it is very difficult to separate ourselves from the conceptual world, and it is only by practice that we can separate ourselves from this conceptual world.

While you are in the world, even if you are fully enlightened, you have to address people by their names because you are here. Even though you have the experience of mentality and materiality, you still have to call everyone by their names. While we live in the world, we cannot separate ourselves from this conventional truth. As long as this body is here, we will have to use all those concepts because this world runs on nothing but concepts, all conventional truths, and we use them in our day-to-day life. No one can get away from concepts; even the enlightened beings call others by their names.

Once you have the experience of mind and matter, once you know that this is the reality, then you are no longer so attached and you no longer have a false view of the world. Once you know the reality, that you are not "I" or "mine," that you are mind and matter; once you have the realization of that, false view is transformed into right view. The personal identity is transformed into right view, wherein you know that there is no man or woman, there is only mentality and materiality. Immediately you know that you have gotten rid of the wrong view, that it has been transformed into the right view. Once you can transform the false view into the right view, that is, that personal identity of "I," "me," and "mine," if you can transform or eliminate it, then you have the right view. Once you have the right view, then you will never enter into the four woeful worlds, that is, the four lowest planes of existence, and that is the happiest thing one can achieve by knowing mentality and materiality. The experience of mentality and materiality is the sure way for you to avoid those four planes of existence which are called woeful. With your practice you will be able to experience the reality of *na-yo*, *nama-rupa*, mentality-materiality, and once you know that all living beings are mentality and materiality, it means that you will have gotten rid of your wrong view and can escape rebirth in the four lowest planes of existence.

A Powerful Kind of Fasting

August 18, 1978
Translated by Rina Sircar

༄

Practice, at least for a week, the fasting known as *eka-tani patabai*, which means sitting in one place with one vessel and eating just once in the whole day. In the afternoon take as much juice as you want but no black tea. Even if you do the ordinary fasting prescribed by the Eight Precepts (eating no solid food past noon), keep the *eka-tani patabai* for seven days. It has much greater value than any other fasting.

Three Roots and Three Branches

August 18, 1978
Translated by Rina Sircar

↢

The three wholesome roots of mind are *alobha*, *adosa*, and *amoha*. We can associate them with the three important qualities of life: *dana*, *sila*, and *bhavana*.

Alobha means that you are not greedy for anything. But further, it means that you have a generous mind and that you give without thinking about getting anything back. Thus, it is associated with *dana*, charitable giving.

Adosa means having no ill-will or aversion for anyone. But further, it means protecting yourself and others by keeping different kinds of precepts for the purpose of bodily purification and discipline. Thus it is associated with *sila*, moral observance.

Amoha means not having dullness or being in illusion, but having knowledge. Further, it means practicing meditation to gain insight into the real nature of things. Thus, it is associated with *bhavana*, mental culture.

Find Your Type

August 18, 1978
Translated by Rina Sircar

ॐ

There are four different types of people who have trouble meditating: those who are very talkative; those who are too sociable and cannot stay alone; those who are sluggish and tired; and those who are always very busy and have no spare time.

What Makes a Meditation?

August 18, 1978
Translated by Rina Sircar

ॐ

When you know that you are having greed, you are no longer in ignorance but possess knowledge.

If you know that you are angry, and have hatred, you are no longer in ignorance but possess knowledge.

When you know that you are having ignorance, that knowing becomes knowledge and it is a meditation.

Even if you become aware of the feeling, "I don't want to meditate," that means you have the insight that you don't want to meditate. Since you know that you do not want to meditate, that knowing becomes the meditation—the mindfulness and awareness that you know what you don't want to do.

Gold Pots and Snakes

June 23, 1983
Translated by Rina Sircar

༄

If you engage in goodness, then you will get a gold pot, but if you engage in evil, then you will get snakes!

There are three kinds of gold pots and there are three different kinds of snakes.

What are the snakes? The three snakes are greed, hatred, and delusion. If these snakes bite, then death is definite. There are two different kinds of snakebite. The real animal snake can kill you with just one bite. But the other snakes—the snakes of greed, hatred, and delusion—will go on biting you throughout your life; it will be continuous biting. If we kill, we have been bitten by the three snakes. If we steal, it is because we have been bitten by the three snakes. As soon as there is killing or stealing, these three poisonous snakes are around and they have bitten you. If we bring unhappiness in somebody's life, or if we tell a lie, it is because of the biting of the poisonous snakes. If we take any kind of liquor or drugs, it is because the three snakes are biting.

The snake Greed is a small one; the Hatred snake is one hundred times bigger than the Greed snake; and the snake Ignorance is a thousand times bigger than the Hatred snake. So one snake is bigger than the other.

With regards to the gold pots, the first one is non-greed, *alobha*. Now what is non-greed? If you do charitable work, if you help or do a meritorious deed, this is called *dana*. Wherever there is charitable work going on, it is an example of the gold pot *alobha*.

The second gold pot is non-hatred, *adosa*, which means having no aversion, and even more important, observing virtues *(sila)* like the Five Precepts, the Eight Precepts, or the Ten Precepts for the sake of oneself and others.

The third gold pot is non-delusion, *amoha*, which means taking up meditation *(bhavana)* by practicing mindfulness which leads to seeing the truth.

To sum up, there are three gold pots: the first one is the gold pot of *dana;* the second gold pot, which is a thousand times bigger than the first, is observing all the virtues, *sila;* and the third is the gold pot of *bhavana*, which is one hundred thousand times bigger than the other gold pots. Try for the gold pots—don't go for the snakebites.

To bring peace on earth, people have to try for the gold pot of *sila:* to abstain from killing, stealing, from misuse of the senses, from telling lies, and from intoxicants. All of us have to try to put these virtues into practice so there will not be any kind of nuclear war or any kind of holocaust or mass destruction of any kind.

Do you know about King Sakka? There are four directions—north, south, east, and west—and in the middle is Mt. Meru. Mt. Meru is 54,000 feet high, and when the sun is going around Mt. Meru, we get the day. When the sun goes around the back of Mt. Meru, then it is dark. This is how we get night and day.

King Sakka was the Universal Monarch of the Four Directions. His kingdom was so big that when the sun rotated around Mt. Meru, in the north kingdom there was day, and when it moved to the other side, the south side, it was night; that is how big the kingdom was.

The king's people liked to visit him and pay their respects, but King Sakka, who was extremely righteous, always said, "I don't want any of this; instead I want all of you to keep the Five Precepts. This is my only request. You don't have to give me respect, you don't have to give me anything, just keep the Five Precepts." Because the king was like that, during his lifetime the kingdom was safe for everyone; everyone was living a righteous life, there was no burglary, no fights, no trouble of any kind. If a person died in Sakka's kingdom, they never used to be reborn in a woeful plane of existence because they had observed the Five Precepts.

So that we will be happy in the future, so that there will be peace and nothing will worry us, and so that we will have a higher birth in the next life, why not keep these Five Virtues?

It is even better if you combine the Five Virtues with mindfulness practice; there is a great deal of benefit in this. The most important benefit is this: while one is being mindful and observing precepts, one is protecting oneself. One does not harm oneself nor others. In this way, the one who is being mindful with precepts also protects others.

Seven Factors of Enlightenment

October 8, 1983

Translated by U Jotika

ॐ

Once a monk asked the Buddha what is meant by a stupid, dumb, and foolish person. And the Buddha said, "Whoever does not practice the Seven Factors of Enlightenment is called stupid, dumb, and foolish."

Once a monk asked the Buddha what he meant by a poor person. The Buddha said, "Whoever does not practice the Seven Factors of Enlightenment is called a poor person, even though a person may have a lot of wealth, nevertheless, they are no different from a poor person if they do not practice the Seven Factors of Enlightenment." Even though a person knows all the scriptures by heart, they are still poor if they do not practice the Seven Factors of Enlightenment.

Everyone should know clearly the Five Hindrances and the Seven Factors of Enlightenment. The first factor is mindfulness; the second is investigation of Dhamma; the third is energy or effort; the fourth, rapture; the fifth, tranquility; the sixth, one-pointedness of mind; and the seventh is equanimity.

The Hindrance of Sensual Desire

September 17, 1983

Translated by U Jotika

༄

Of the Five Hindrances to meditation, sensual desire is the first. The Buddha said, "Monks, as this body depends on nourishment, so it is that these Five Hindrances live on nourishment. Without nourishment, they cannot arise and cannot live on."

What is the nourishment for the arising of the hindrances and for their continuing to arise? It is unwise thinking. When you see something or hear something, usually you think it is permanent, it will bring happiness, and that there is somebody there who is enjoying and seeing it, and that it is beautiful.

For greed to arise, the sign of beauty is the nourishment. If a person thinks of something as nice, as beautiful, greed for that thing will arise. If we keep on thinking of those things as nice or beautiful, this greed will come again and again, and will persist.

Everyone wants to see something very nice, wants to hear something very nice, wants to smell something very nice, and eat good food. It is greed that wants these things, and most people think that if they get want they want, then greed will be satisfied. But in truth this is not so. The more we get, the more we want. Greed is like a wild animal; if you feed a wild animal you cannot drive him away. Even though you try to drive him away with sticks and stones, he will not go away. So it is with greed. If we "feed" sensual pleasures to the wild animal of greed, it will never go away, it will become stronger and stronger. Most people think that if we have some desire, the best thing to do is to act, to go and do something to satisfy the desire, but this is not necessarily so.

Usually when a person wants to see something like a movie or TV he does so without hesitation. If you watch your desires with mindfulness, however, you will see that desires are impermanent. The same is true for all sensual pleasures: if you watch them, you will find nothing permanent; they are not "me" or "mine."

The best way to deal with greed is to see it as impermanent, to see that it doesn't really bring happiness, and to see that pleasures are not substantial, not "I," "me," or "mine." It is not good either to indulge or suppress the desire. The best way is simply to watch the desire and see deeply into the nature of desire, which is accompanied by suffering of its loss.

If, out of habit, you think that something is permanent, pleasurable, or beautiful, the desire which has not arisen will arise, and the desire which has arisen will become stronger and stronger. But if you see that things are impermanent and that your attachment to them can bring suffering, if you see that our bodies have the aspect of repulsiveness, those desires will not come. The desire that is there will go away, and the desire which has not arisen will not arise. By being mindful, we are not feeding the wild beast of greed. Those who practice meditation and keep the Precepts put a limit to greed. Eventually, the grasping nature of the mind weakens.

The Precepts are like the ground. Anyone who has to do work has to stand on the ground firmly. So when you practice meditation, observe the Precepts. Your mind will become much stronger and you will feel much happier. Keeping the Precepts helps support meditation and not greed. When you practice meditation, you have to be willing to do everything that will support meditation. If you really practice, you will see the truth.

Whatever we see, hear, smell, taste—if we watch mindfully, we will see the impermanence, the suffering, the soulless quality, we will see the superficial nature of beauty. If we continuously watch like this, then greed for these things will go away. If you understand this, you will get relief from desire and sensual pleasure; if you don't, then you will go on suffering.

A human being or a *deva*—anybody who is practicing meditation—can be called *bhikkhu* (monk). Why can he or she be called *bhikkhu?* Because that person is destroying greed, destroying hatred, and destroying delusion. *Bhikkhu* in another way means someone who is engaged in destroying ignorance. You can lead a worldly life, and still develop a very deep understanding of the truth; you can even become enlightened.

That Bhikkhu who, while still young, devotes himself to the Buddha's Teaching, illumines this world as does the moon freed from a cloud. (Verse 382)

How to Practice Mindfulness

September 17, 1983
Translated by U Jotika

ॐ

Concerning the practice of meditation, the Buddha said, "Disciples, you should practice so that you always live with mindfulness and clear comprehension. Whatever you do, do with mindfulness." The Buddha's cousin, the Venerable Nanda Thera, was very mindful. Likewise should you be also. Whenever you look, look very mindfully; when you are looking straight ahead you must be mindful of that. When you want to look to the side, turn your head slowly, very mindfully. When you bend, bend slowly and mindfully. When you stretch, stretch mindfully. If there is mindfulness, there is also clear comprehension. Live mindfully and with clear comprehension; this is my request to you.

Whenever putting on your clothes, when washing your clothes, or hanging them on the line; whatever you do with your eating vessels, taking your plate, washing it, your silverware—do it very mindfully. Also, when taking a mouthful of food, chewing, and swallowing, be mindful of every action with regard to eating. Whatever you drink, as you reach for the cup, raise the cup, touch the cup to the lips, swallow—be aware of hotness or coldness. Be aware of whether or not there is hardness or softness in the food. When you taste, you must do so mindfully. Be mindful when you are urinating or defecating. When you walk, from the time you pick up your foot and place it down again, be mindful of the lifting, pushing forward, and dropping down of the foot. When you are standing, you must be aware of the posture of your body. Be aware of:

Seeing, hearing, *walking*, touching.

Seeing, hearing, *standing*, touching.

Seeing, hearing, *sitting*, touching.

Seeing, hearing, *lying*, touching.

When falling asleep, be aware that you are falling asleep. When waking up, you should be aware that you are waking up. This is very hard in the beginning. If a person can talk very mindfully, if he is mindful while he is talking, it shows that his mindfulness is very strong. Whenever you want to speak, just remind yourself to speak mindfully, and say, "If I cannot speak mindfully, then I won't speak." So, be very careful when you speak. When you are silent, then you should be aware that you are silent, and note, "silent, silent, silent."

When you see, see as much as you can, and be aware of as many things as you can; don't concentrate only on one object. Your mind should see more, should be aware of more; in this way your mindfulness will become strong. When you hear something, listen very mindfully, the more you can hear the better it is. Without any choosing or rejecting, try to be aware of all the sounds around you. Be aware of many sounds; when you practice this for a long time you will hear a kind of sound that is inside your ear. At first it is very subtle, and if you are aware of that, keep your mindfulness there, and the sound will become louder and louder. Whatever smell you sense, you must be aware of that; you should note it as "smelling, smelling, smelling." Whether or not it is pleasant, you must be aware of it.

There are many touching points on your body where you feel touching; there is touching your clothes, touching the floor, etc. Whatever touching sensations there are you must be aware of them. First you should be aware of the most obvious touching sensation. Then you should try to be aware of the touching sensations over the whole body.

When you practice mindfulness like this, the mind will become calm and quiet. The mind will stay in the present moment, and you will have concentration. Only with concentration can you see things as they are. If you can keep your mind on whatever object you want to, if your mind stays there, this shows that your mind is settled and concentrated. If you have concentration, then you will know the truth, you will know things as they are. So try to keep your mind on one object.

To get good results, you should practice meditation the whole day. You should practice during the first watch of the night, from 6:00 to 10:00 PM. Then you should sleep from 10:00 PM to 2:00 AM and from that time, from 2:00 to 6:00 AM, you should practice meditation, and on into the day without interruption. If you can practice like this then you will get results very quickly. Put your effort in practice. Only by practicing continuously without a break will you get good results. If your practice is interrupted frequently, it is very hard to achieve concentration.

Meditating with the Elements

August 16, 1978
Translated by Rina Sircar

ॐ

We should be aware of the four material elements: earth, water, fire, and air, and the four secondary elements: color, shape, or form; smell; taste; and nutriment.

You will find these eight elements in any object; invariably, they are in every object. These are the most important elements, and every object has them.

In order to see the four primary elements, you have to meditate on the body along with the four main elements. You have to say, "I am the earth, I am the water, I am the heat, I am the air." When you do that, you will at once know the solidity of the body, the fluidity of this body, the heat of this body, and the air or movement of this body.

We always feel this "I" very strongly. If you want to see beyond this "I" you can say, "I am the earth, I am the water, I am the fire, I am the air." You can extend this meditation to other people by saying, "There is the earth, there is the water, there is the fire, there is the air." Then you see in that person all the essential elements; you will see that they are all earth, air, fire, and water. So where is the "I?" Where is "he?" Where is "she?" Where are "they?" Because of "I," we see man as man, woman as woman.

Meditate on the four sets of noble postures *(iriya po leba)*:
Seeing, hearing, *standing*, touching;
Seeing, hearing, *walking*, touching;
Seeing, hearing, *sitting*, touching;
Seeing, hearing, *lying*, touching.

If we keep our concentration strong we can easily realize that there is nothing but earth, water, fire, and air. Even when we breathe in and breathe out and are aware of touching, we can feel the solidity, the liquidity, the temperature, and the movement of the body. So, when we meditate on the four sets of noble actions we can easily realize that there are eight things that are very important to understanding our meditation. Besides this, there is nothing. Even when we breathe in and breathe out, we can easily feel the solidity of the body, the liquidity of the body, the heat of the body, and the motion of the body.

Regarding the secondary elements, we can never see, smell, taste, or receive nourishment. But we can see shape, form, and color. So when you are watching your sitting, you are watching the materiality. It is too difficult to see air, heat, and motion. Only when the meditation becomes very good can you touch everything, like the earth, and you can also touch heat and you can feel air, but you cannot touch water. You will be touching the heat or cold of the water, you will feel the temperature of the water.

By knowing the *nama-rupa* of all things we can get rid of our attachments. At first, we are so attached to this body, to this person or that person, but actually if we analyze them according to the four primary and four secondary elements, then we will gradually know there is no "I-ness."

Truth and Mind

August 20, 1978

Translated by Rina Sircar

ॐ

From the Buddhist point of view everything is given a name, but these names are mere concepts and exist for the purpose of structure, for the sole purpose of convenience. Names are given, but "man," "woman," and all the names of the animals—these are all just conventional truth.

There is also an ultimate truth which consists of mentality and materiality. All sentient beings are nothing but mentality and materiality, but we give each one a name, which is a concept and represents the sentient being, but is not the real being. Therefore, there is the distinction between the ultimate *(parama)* and the conventional *(pannyati)*. When we say "man," "woman," "dog," "horse," "chair," "table," when we try to label everything, then these become conventional truths, but they are not absolute truths.

Absolute truth is the truth which includes *na-yo*—mentality and materiality. These two are the only ultimate truths. *Na*, mentality, is composed of consciousness, what we call the mind, and mental factors. *Yo*, materiality, is composed of earth, water, air, and fire, and also form or shape or color, smell, taste, and nourishment or nutriment. These are the eight materialities. Mind or consciousness cannot stand on its own. It must be supported by the mental factors or the psychic factors. Our consciousness is constantly colored by the mental factors or the psychic factors.

Therefore, when we say "man," "woman," "house," "horse," and "dog," these are conventional truths. The real truth is the ultimate truth, that everything we view is actually only mentality and materiality.

"What is meant by mentality?"

The consciousness and the mental factors.

"What are the mental factors?"

Regarding the mental factors, our mind, as it is, is very tender. It is so clean that as it is pure mind, we cannot know what it is. Only when it is colored by the mental factors, then the mind comes up and we know, "this is consciousness." Actually consciousness, or the mind, is pure and light, and so it needs its support, or it cannot stay. Its supports are the mental factors, such as greed, hatred, and delusion (the root unwholesome mental factors), and also generosity, good will, knowledge, and wisdom or insight (examples of wholesome mental factors). So, when consciousness and mental factors arise together, we can understand mind quite clearly. Because of our will, because of our volition, we perform different actions. Therefore, because of one volition *(cetana)*, there is one life. Each volition is one *bhava*, one life. We act in the world from volition, therefore we have to come back to this life. One volition equals one life.

"Are the mental factors what cause the mind to arise and become active?"

Yes, the mind becomes very active because of these mental factors. Without them the mind is very passive; it is inactive. Because of these mental factors our mind becomes angry, our mind has sloth and torpor, our mind has hatred and aversion. There are also wholesome mental factors, such as mindfulness, confidence, and faith.

"This teaching says that just by knowing unwholesome mental factors, knowledge arises and the unwholesome mental factors cease. Why is this so?"

When you have greed, if you at once know, "I have greed, I have greed," this means that you have placed the mental factor of mindfulness on your greed, and at that moment you are not greedy in an unconscious way. Greed, accompanied by mindfulness, becomes a kind of knowledge, and with that knowledge greed slowly gives way to non-greed. It is same with anger—if you do not know that you are angry, then it is a kind of ignorance; once you know that you are angry, it means you are mindful about your anger. When you know that you are angry, then with that knowledge the anger gives way to non-anger.

"But does that mean that the greed would necessarily disappear? Wouldn't there still need to be some kind of will-power not to be greedy at that point?"

Yes, which means you are meditating at that point. It shows that you are mindful that you are greedy, and so when you know that you are greedy, your greed becomes less and less, and you will develop a distaste for your own greed. When I know that I am angry, I should try to control my anger. But as long as I do not know I am angry, my temper continues. It depends on how far you know what you are doing. If you do not know, that means that again you have to stay in the vicious circle and come back. But if you know, and you are controlling, then you are progressing, you are cutting your ignorance and increasing your knowledge.

Take, for example, *alobha*—generosity—when you practice this, it is wholesome, and it is a kind of *dana*—charitable giving, or doing good work. *Adosa* means good will. This means you are trying to keep up some of the disciplines of your life; you are keeping the Five Precepts, or the Eight Precepts, or the Ten Precepts. This is a kind of bodily purification. And *amoha* can be compared with meditation, different kinds of meditation such as insight meditation *(vipassana)*.

There are other factors which create hindrances to our meditation. There are three obstacles, and the three together create a very big hindrance to our spiritual progress: *tanha*, which is craving; *mana*, which is conceit; and *ditthi*, which is false view, the false view that believes one can progress spiritually by performing lots of sacrifices and external rituals. So one should be very careful not to have any of these three on our way, as they are the greatest hindrances or poisons. These three are also mental factors.

Another obstacle is *mucchariya*, or stinginess, which means you feel very unhappy to give to others. This is the opposite of *dana*, or charitable giving.

Wherever there is hatred, there is delusion. So with any of the bad roots, delusion will always be accompanying the others. If you want to kill anything, that is *dosa*, hatred; and if you want to steal something, that is *lobha*, greed. These two are always accompanied by *moha*, delusion.

When we ask, "Which is there more of, ignorance or knowledge?" Of course, there is much more ignorance than knowledge. In this world we do everything with ignorance, and we do very little with mindfulness. When we drink, we are not aware of our drinking; so also, with our eating, what we are eating and how we are eating, we are not mindful about that. This is all because of *moha*, which is the same as ignorance.

Memorize this little verse to help you remember:
Lobha, dosa, moha: akudo mula taya tonba.
Alobha, adosa, amoha: kudo mula taya tonba.

The meaning is this: Greed, hatred, and delusion: these are the three unwholesome roots. Non-greed, non-hatred, non-delusion: these are the three wholesome roots.

Altogether there are six roots, three wholesome and three unwholesome. The three unwholesome roots can be compared in the following way: if one steals, the stealing is accompanied by a lot of greed, and if one kills, the killing is accompanied by a lot of ill will and hatred. In these two acts, *moha*, or ignorance, is always present.

The three wholesome roots are *alobha*—charity, giving with an open heart and not expecting anything back; and *adosa*, meaning bodily purification such as when you observe the Five, Eight, or Ten Precepts. The Precepts refer to *sila*, moral observances.

Once you achieve bodily purification, there is *amoha*—which means one is quite ready for *bhavana*, or meditation for mental purification.

When you meditate, the mind is very difficult to control, even for a very short period. So, whenever we do meditation, the mind comes up with different kinds of mental factors, such as conceit—this is mentality; or greed—this is also mentality. Mind comes up with anger—this is also mentality. It is not "I" which is getting angry, it is not "I" which is having conceit. It is not "I" which is having a lot of greed, it is mentality; it is because of mentality. Our mind is always covered by the different mental factors—anger, or greed, or hatred, or conceit. None of these is "I." When anger comes up, it is not an "I" who is experiencing anger, for the "I" is *pannyati*—conventional truth; it is a label. *Na*, or mind, is experiencing anger, and mind is one aspect of ultimate truth.

There is a distinction between the two different kinds of truth: one is *pannyati tissa*, which is conventional truth; the other is *paramata tissa*, ultimate truth which consists of consciousness, mental factors, materiality, and *nibbana*. Besides these four, everything else is also true, but only from the conventional point of view. There are four other truths which can also be considered ultimate truth, or *paramata tissa*—suffering, the origin of suffering, the cessation of suffering, and the path leading to the cessation of suffering. These are commonly called The Four Noble Truths.

"Can you elaborate on the distinctions between ultimate realities and ultimate truths?"

The four ultimate realities are consciousness, mental factors, matter, and *nibbana*. If you try to analyze the four ultimate realities, you will see that they belong to the Four Noble Truths. The first two ultimate realities—conciousness and mental factors—and the third ultimate reality—materiality—belong to the First Noble Truth, the truth of suffering. The first two ultimate realities also belong to the Second Noble Truth, the cause of the suffering, because craving is the cause of suffering and it is one of the mental factors. The fourth ultimate reality, *nibbana*, belongs to the Third and Fourth Noble Truths, which are the cessation of suffering and the path out of our suffering.

Unwholesome Conducts, Sainthood, and Nibbana

August 24, 1978
Translated by Rina Sircar

ॐ

Kamma-Patha, "Course of Action," is a name for the group
of ten kinds of either unwholesome or wholesome actions.

In Buddhist ethics there are ten unwholesome conducts. Three of these unwholsome conducts proceed from our body, and are called *kaya-kan*. The conducts particular to our body door cannot be done with our speech or with our thoughts. The *kaya-kan* are taking life, stealing, and sexual misconduct.

There are four unwholesome conducts associated with our speech door, and these are called *wezi-kan*. These four cannot be performed either with our bodily actions nor with our thoughts. The four *wezi-kan* are telling lies, slandering, rude speech, and foolish talk, such as gossip or flattery.

If we analyze the mind door, we find three unwholesome conducts we perform with our mind, called *mano-kan*. They are envy, hatred or aversion, and wrong view. So there are ten different kinds of *kan*, of which we can again say that of these ten, three are under *kaya-kan*, four are under *wezi-kan*, and three are under *mano-kan*.

If we chant these ten unwholesome conducts, we say:
Panatipata, adenadana, kametumessasara, kaya-kan tonba.
Mutawada, pitunawassa, brutawassa, tampampalampa, wezi-kan leba.
Awesa, vyapada, mesadetthi, mano-kan tonba.
Kaya-kan tonba, wezi-kan leba, mano-kan tonba—alone dusaria seba.

In English they are:

Killing, stealing, sexual misconduct, these are three unwholesome conducts of the body door.

Lying, slandering, rude speech, foolish talk—these are the four unwholesome conducts of the speech-door.

Envy, hatred, wrong view—these are the three unwholesome conducts of the mind-door.

Three from the body-door, four from the speech-door, three from the mind door—altogether there are ten unwholesome conducts.

Because of the ten unwholesome *kan* we get unwholesome results. As you sow, so shall you reap. So, if you steal, kill, have envy, and so on, you will experience the suffering you have caused others.

There also are the opposite conducts which are wholesome. For example, charity, keeping good moral discipline, doing meditation, having right views about things, right concentration, and right mindfulness. We group these good conducts into three sections: *dana*, *sila*, and *bhavana*. As there are unwholesome conducts which bring unwholesome results, so also performing meritorious deeds, having a self-sacrificing nature, having good will toward others, and doing a lot of meditation practice—these are the wholesome conducts. And they will also give us good results. Because of the good wholesome thoughts, words, and deeds, the results will also be wholesome.

The Attainment of Stages

In Buddhist psychology, there are three unwholesome roots, and because of these we have to come back many times. These three roots—*lobha*, *dosa*, *moha* (greed, hatred, delusion)—cause pain and suffering and all the different negative fields. To get rid of these three, we have to meditate and we have to practice a lot. Because of these three, we can never find happiness and we can never get peace. To get rid of these three, we will have to practice a lot, so that instead of greed *(lobha)*, we will practice self-sacrifice *(alobha)*. *Dosa* will become *adosa;* from ill-will we will develop good-will. And *moha*, which is delusion, a kind of ignorance—due to your practice this will be replaced by insight *(amoha)*.

If we want to attain the stage of streamwinner *(sotapanna)*, we will have to get rid of six out of ten unwholesome conducts—all three *kaya-kan* (killing, stealing, and sexual misconduct); from *wezi-kan* we will have to get rid of two: telling lies and using abusive words or slander; and from *mano-kan* we will have to get rid of wrong views. If we can get rid of these six, we can attain the first stage of sainthood called the streamwinner stage.

"How will we know if we have attained a stage?"

Others may not know that you have attained a stage, but only you can know.

If you want to attain the second stage of sainthood, the once-returner stage *(sakadagami)*, then you will have to weaken all the ten unwholesome conducts. When you become a streamwinner, you have already gotten rid of six. Say you went from the size of a human being who is carrying a heavy load to the size of a fly. This is the difference between being an ordinary person with the ten unwholesome conducts and being a person who has attained the first stage of sainthood and has gotten rid of six unwholesome conducts. When you become a once-returner, you have become as light as the legs of that fly.

To attain the third level of sainthood, the never-returner *(anagami)*, we will have to get rid of the ten bad conducts almost completely. There will still be a little bit of delusion and a little bit of greed. When one attains the final stage, that is, the *arahat* stage, all these ten will be totally gone. And then the *arahat* attains *nibbana*.

The Two Stages of Nibbana

Did you know that in *nibbana* there are exquisite carpets, delicious food, and beautiful trees?

There are two different stages of *nibbana*. The first stage is *Tha u pa di the ta neban;* the person has attained *nibbana* but is still alive, and still has the body which consists of the Five Groups *(panca khanda):* materiality *(rupa)*, feeling *(vedana)*, perception *(sanna)*, mental formations *(sankhara)*, and consciousness *(vinnana)*. These five are still there, and the person experiences different kinds of thoughts, painful or pleasurable sensations, and feelings. But these are all experienced without any attachment. Also, equanimity takes the place of mental pain and happiness. From time to time, as long as the body is there, there is the desire to eat, the desire to do certain things, but everything is done without attachment. As this enlightened person still has a body, so they will have to do all the things necessary to keep it up, until they drop the body. So, with the first stage of *nibbana*, one has to do everything, but one's speech, thoughts, and actions are beyond greed, hatred, and delusion, and are carried out without attachment for anything.

There is no greater moment than the attainment of the first stage of *nibbana*. In fact, out of all the different moments possible, this moment is the most important moment in the whole universe.

This is the first stage of *nibbana, tha u pa di the ta neban,* the *nibbana* remaining with the physical bases.

The second stage of *nibbana* is called *anu pa di the ta neban*—the *nibbana* remaining without the bases; that is, the enlightened mind and the body are separated. But even then, something remains. It is the Third Noble Truth—*Nirodha*—the Cessation of Suffering. All the other Noble Truths are gone. Secondly, there is the *dhamma ayatana*—the truth base; and thirdly, there is the *dhamma dhatu*—the truth element. In this stage of *nibbana*, the "person"—the

Five Khandas— is no longer there, and there are no more plea-sureable or painful states. The whole cycle of *na-yo* is controlled. This is the second stage of *nibbana—anu pa di the ta neban*.

In the *Questions of King Milinda*, there is a great dialogue between the king and the wisest man of that time whose name was Nagasena. King Milinda doubted Nagasena: "You have given me so many dif-ferent definitions of *nibbana*, but how do I know whether there is any *nibbana* or not?" So Nagasena said, "O King, you talk about wind, but is there any wind?" The king said, "Without wind, how can I breathe?" "But," Nagasena replied, "I don't see any wind." The king said, "You don't see the wind, but you are breathing, even though I don't see the wind, I see you breathing, and I know that you are alive." "So also," said Nagasena, "*nibbana* is something like the wind. You cannot see it, but it is there."

All of us are breathing, but none of us can see the breath of one another. So also in the same way, no one can see *nibbana*, but we can experience *nibbana*. As you can experience breath, so you can experience *nibbana* even though you cannot see it. Please try very hard to attain these stages.

Uprooting the Roots

August 21, 1978
Translated by Rina Sircar

࿐

There are different techniques for meditation, and there are many different objects which can be taken for our concentration. Breathing in and breathing out is a very important one to do first in order to develop our concentration. For developing our concentration we should always try to get rid of greed, hatred, and delusion, because these three are the greatest obstacles in our mind. To calm our mind, we should practice mindfulness of breathing. Only when we can get rid of greed, hatred, and delusion do the other qualities become strong. To have a wholesome mind, we must get rid of the unwholesome root.

It is always important for all of us to practice mindfulness. To practice mindfulness, different objects are given. Here the emphasis is on breathing in and breathing out. It is the most important basic practice to start with. Only when we achieve concentration can we get rid of the three great obstacles, the three hindrances on our way.

It is very difficult to develop our concentration because our mind is rooted in the unwholesome roots. Now, to get rid of these three roots takes lot of time. To start with, the most basic and most important meditation instruction is simply breathing in and breathing out. When we start our meditation, it is very difficult to control our mind, and when we are trying to get our concentration we will experience the three unwholesome roots trying to arise. But once greed comes up and the mind is colored with this greed, and when I know that it has come up, instead of fighting against it, instead of doing anything reactive, I say, "I'm greedy, I'm greedy, I'm greedy." Then it is very easy to get rid of it.

Also, when anger comes up in the mind and I say, "I'm angry, I'm angry," when I know that I am angry, the anger can never stay. Gradually, the anger will go away, and good-will will come.

In the same way, if I know that I am in delusion, I will have to say, "I'm in delusion, I'm in delusion." Gradually the delusion will go away. Very slowly all the unwholesome roots will go away.

When we sit for our practice the mind is difficult to control because the mind always likes to wander. When the mind is wandering, it is better not to fight with it, but just make a mental note, "Mind is wandering, mind is wavering." At that moment, you will find that the mind is calming down, and you will be able to gain control over the mind.

If I see that my mind is wandering and I fight it, my mind will wander more. So instead of fighting and reacting, just acknowledge the wandering. Then knowledge arises. Also sometimes it happens that we are sitting for our practice, but due to our sluggishness, due to our sloth and torpor, due to our laziness, our mind goes far away. This is due to sluggishness. At that time, we must again bring our mind back. In this way, instead of fighting, instead of reacting, we must say, "I'm lazy, I'm lazy." When you know that you are lazy, it is no longer ignorance, it is knowledge. Your mind is no longer lazy, there is insight present, and gradually you can control your mind.

Where is Kennedy?

August 21, 1978
Translated by Rina Sircar

꒰

In Buddhist psychology, there are four ultimate realities, and these four are the mind, mental factors, materiality, and *nibbana*.

Sometimes we give names like "sheep," "goat," "man," "woman," and when we give names, we are assigning concepts. The reality is the mentality and materiality, but when we give names and label things, they are just concepts, they are not actually what is real. They are a kind of delusion. When we analyze them, we find they are composed of mentality and materiality.

Is "Kennedy" in mentality and materiality?

Is "Kennedy" different from mentality and materiality?

Is there mentality and materiality in "Kennedy"?

Is "Kennedy" permanently there?

These questions explain to us that the name "Kennedy" is still there; it is a concept, a name that will be always there. But actually, who we called "Kennedy" was made up of mentality and materiality, and this is gone.

All these names create a view of personal identity. Once we can understand mentality and materiality in a correct way, then we will see that beyond mentality and materiality there is only a label. This is *dhammaditthi:* the knowledge that the individual is composed of mentality and materiality.

The name, whatever name we give, lives on in memory as an abstract concept, but actually a person is made up of mentality-materiality, and when that person dies, the mentality and materiality separate from each other. But the name which is a concept will always be there while the reality which makes up the person is gone at death. The name "Kennedy" is still there, but he is no longer there, the mentality-materiality is gone.

In mentality and materiality, there cannot be a name, and in a name there cannot be mentality-materiality, that is, Kennedy. The mentality-materiality is one thing, and the name given is something else.

Two Buddhas, Sumedha and Dipankara, lived long, long ago. Today their names are still here, but their mentality and materiality are no more. The names will always be there, long after the mind and body are gone.

Who Am I?

August 21, 1978
Translated by Rina Sircar

꒰

We are always thinking "I," "mine," "we," "they," "he," "she," "man," "woman," but when we analyze we will find that there is no "man" nor "woman," there is no other thing than mentality and materiality. We are made up of mentality and materiality; mental states and material elements. What is this material and mental phenomena? The mental phenomena—when you see a man or a woman—is nothing but *na*, mind. Mind cannot exist by itself. Mind needs support. Mind by itself, or consciousness by itself, is nothing. It is very clean, but it has its own support, the mental states, the psychic factors. Therefore, in all of us, whether we are man or woman or whether we are animal, all of us have the same *na*, which is mind plus mental factors. The *yo* is materiality. There is no such thing as man, and there is no such thing as woman. We are merely material elements.

When we say, "I am meditating," actually "I" am not meditating, but mentality-materiality is meditating. When we say that "I am eating," who is eating? It is the mentality-materiality that is eating. It is the mind that commands the matter to follow its orders, because matter by itself is nothing; it has no control. The mind and its mental factors control materiality.

It is not the body that is eating, it is the mind which wants to eat, therefore the body is getting the food. It is not that the body wants to meditate, but the mind which commands the body to meditate. It is not the body which wants to do this or that; it is the mind which controls the body or the matter.

In Praise of the Mettaya (Maitreya) Buddha

჻

For the Mettaya to appear
Try to make your heart clean and peaceful
So that the Mettaya will blossom sooner.
In the days of King Rama
People were so loyal, and they were very one-pointed
On a single path.
During the time of the King of Kosala
There was the Sasana Era.
Also, the time of Abhiboona was the time
Of the Sasana Era.
In the time of Dighasani, people used to meditate

Good is the sight of the Ariyas; their company is ever happy....
(Verse 206)

For the reappearance of the Sasana.
The simple Brahmin Sinki also meditated
One-pointedly for the appearance of a Buddha.
Another famous Brahmin, Saddhya, also meditated
One-pointedly for the appearance of the Mettaya.
Even the celestial elephant Nalagiri, for the preservation
Of the Sasana, did not kill the Buddha.
All this has been preserved for the Mettaya to appear.
For the Mettaya to appear, people have to love
Each other many, many years.
They have to maka a pagoda which is 8,000 half-arm lengths.
There is a Bodhi tree which has been growing for the last 240 years
To embrace the Mettaya.
Then, for the Mettaya to sit, make a throne
Which should be sixty-four half-arms' length.
When the whole universe will be one, when there will not be
Any direction like north, east, south, or west,
Only then will the Sasana reappear.
When the whole universe will have love
Which has no discrimination,
Then the Mettaya will appear.
Only in this way, when there will be love for all the sentient beings,
Then Mettaya Phaya will be right in front of us.
When there will be love for the truth,
When there will be love for the Sangha,
And the Sangha will love all the living beings,
Then it will be an unusual time full of love and compassion
Where suffering will be washed away.
At that time the Mettaya will appear.
So, all sentient beings, especially human beings—
Have strength, be one-pointed, and try to bring
The Mettaya into your mind first.

The Peacock and the Dog

༃

O yogis, you should be like the peacock and not like the dog. In nature, you have most likely seen both baby peacocks and puppies. Which is more lovable? As the baby peacock is brown and without any feathers, you would probably say the puppy is more lovable.

But once the peacock is fully grown it has a beautiful blue body and a fan of many colors. However, as it ages the dog loses its fur and suffers from ticks and fleas.

Similarly, you must practice *sila* (virtue), *samadhi* (concentration), and *panna* (wisdom) in order to avoid the forlorn fate of an old dog. The continual practice of these three results in spiritual illumination that is like the beautiful royal blue plumage of the full-grown peacock. If you fulfill *sila*, *samadhi*, and *panna*, everyone will love you, and you will love yourself as well.

For Those Who Practice
Sitting Meditation

჻

If you keep your hands and feet in one position for a long time, you will experience all kinds of feelings at every moment.

In your mind you will not achieve one-pointedness, your meditation will not go anywhere, and you will not get the most important thing.

On the path which is wholesome, there are no feelings to call painful.

Whenever you have to move, move. With no painful feelings in the mind, the mind will get one-pointedness, the meditation will progress, and the results will be great.

Have Confidence in The Buddha

ॐ

Have confidence in the Buddha,
And you cannot make a mistake, they say.

You will not be reborn in the four miserable abodes for 100,000
world cycles, if you have love, respect, and have confidence in him.

By way of your own devotion, you can reach the *deva loka*
As if you are being lifted up by your own hand.

You are very sure to be reborn in the human or *deva* world;
This is your firm destiny.

Through your devotion, you will become a streamwinner.

Darkness

སྲ

Midnight is dark.
The new moon is dark.
The thickness of the forest is dark.
But darkest of all is ignorance.

The Cause of Suffering

That which you cannot conquer is *anicca* (impermanence).
Because you cannot conquer it, there is *dukkha* (suffering).

Dependent Origination

If you know, it will break.
If you do not know, you will go around and around:
This is dependent origination.

How to Achieve World Peace

༃

If I do everything with awareness, then the whole lot of "I"s will be aware, too. If I am mindful, then all around me will be mindful; the whole village will be mindful, then the whole world. If I am mindful, then you must be mindful if you are around me. If I am mindful, you cannot disturb me. If I am always mindful, and you are around me, how long can you remain unmindful?

How to Practice

✥

Eat less, sleep less, read less, talk less.

The Efficacy of Sarana-Gamana

A Discourse by the Very Venerable
Taungpulu Tawya Kaba-Aye Sayadaw
Interpreted by Rina Sircar

ॐ

There are many benefits to *sarana-gamana*, or Taking Refuge in the Three Gems. The Three Gems are the Buddha, the Dhamma, and the Sangha. *Sarana-gamana* is suitable for people of all ages, including children. One can take Refuge at no expense; it is not even strenuous.

Attasamam pemam n'atthi means there is no love like the love of self. Therefore, offering our own self which we love most is the highest and noblest act, and we accumulate the greatest benefit from this act. From the Buddhist point of view, there is nothing higher than this.

The benefits of taking Refuge are great. *Attanam niyyatetva dinnatta sarana-gamanam mahapphalataran ti vuttam.* According to the definition, *Himsati ti saranam,** sarana* is so called because it destroys and eradicates. Now, what does it destroy? It destroys birth in the four woeful planes of existence, such as the plane of hell and the realms of the animals, hungry ghosts, and demons. This *sarana-gamana* (literally, "going to"), or taking Refuge, protects us from physical and psychological suffering. And after death we will have an easy rebirth in the world of *devas*. There are deities in that realm, but they have not taken Refuge. Hence, there is a vast difference between these deities and the deities who enter the *deva loka* after taking Refuge. Those who are born in that plane after taking Refuge are superior to those who haven't taken Refuge.

The deities with Refuge excel the others in ten aspects: *Dibbena ayuna vaunena sukhena yasena adhipateyyena, dibbena rupehi saddehi*

---

* *Anguttara-Nikaya Atthakatha*, Vol. III, p. 272.

*gandhehi rasehi photthabbehi.** The meaning is this: The life span
is celestially long, the being is especially superior in appearance,
great happiness is there, reputation, and sovereignty. These beings
also possess celestial sense-objects of form, sound, smell, taste, and
touch.

> *Etam kho saranam khemam*
> *Etam saranam uttamam*
> *Etam saranam agamma*
> *Sabba dukkha pamuccati.*[†]

The meaning is this: This Refuge is peaceful indeed. This Refuge
is best. If taken, this Refuge frees us from all suffering.

Basically, by taking Refuge in the Three Gems we have protection from all troubles. By taking Refuge, we can attain both
path-consciousness and fruit-consciousness which leads to *nibbana*. Here are some stories to inspire us:

During the Buddha's lifetime, there was a kinsman of the Buddha
who was called Sarana Upasaka because he was so firmly established in the Refuge. But he was also a drunkard who drank just
before dying. When he died, the disciples approached the Buddha
to find out about his next life. The Buddha disclosed that the
man was reborn in the abode of the deities. The other kinsmen
criticized the Buddha, saying, "We cannot believe that a man
who drank his whole lifetime has entered the celestial plane of existence." This became the topic of almost every gathering and meet-
ing.

Hearing this, Prince Mahanama approached the Buddha and
reported that the kinsmen were talking ill about the Buddha.
The Buddha wanted to know the reason. Prince Mahanama said,

---

* *Sakka-Sutta, Salayatana-Samyutta*, p. 469.
† *The Dhammapada*, v. 192.

"Nobody believed when you said that Sarana Upasaka was reborn in the plane of deities." The Buddha answered, "As soon as he died he attained the stage of *sotapanna*, the first stage of sainthood on the way to *nibbana*, and was reborn in the world of deities, a celestial world. The demerit that he may have acquired from drinking could not bar his rebirth in the plane of deities, as the qualities of the Buddha, Dhamma, and Sangha are immeasurable. And he had unshakable faith *(aveccapasada)*. For this reason, the demerit that he accumulated from his drinking was too weak to obstruct him from being reborn as a *deva*."

Regarding Sarana Upasaka's deep faith in the Three Gems, when someone said to him, "O Sarana Upasaka, say that the Buddha is not the Buddha, the Dhamma is not the Dhamma, and the Sangha is not the Sangha. If you do not, I shall behead you," his brave reply was this: "If you have to behead me, do so. I will never say that the Buddha is not the Buddha, the Dhamma is not the Dhamma, and the Sangha is not the Sangha."*

There is an inspiring illustration how unshakable faith in the Three Gems can lead us to realize the Dhamma, even without our putting forth any effort. This story is about a man living in utter poverty, who lived by begging. He had a serious skin disease called leprosy. Someone said to him, "You are so poor, and you have to go around begging for your food. Not only will I give you gold, silver, and other valuables, more than you need for your entire life, but I will also have you cured of your dreadful disease—if you will just say that the Buddha is not the Buddha, the Dhamma is not the Dhamma, and the Sangha is not the Sangha." The poor man replied, "I do not want the riches you offer. Nor do I care whether or not my disease shall be cured. Never shall I say that the Buddha is not the Buddha, the Dhamma is not the Dhamma, and the Sangha is not the Sangha." If we can sacrifice all worldly gain in this

* *Samyutta-Nikaya Atthakatha*, Vol. I, p. 207.

manner, we can also achieve realization of the Dhamma without putting forth any effort.*

The Buddha speaks of two things that we find very difficult to part with.

Dve'ma, bhikkhave, asa duppajaha katama dve? Labhasa ca jivitasa ca imakho, bhikkhave, dve asa duppajaha.†

These, O monks, are two attachments that are hard to give up. What are the two? Attachment to gains and attachment to life. These indeed, O monks, are the two attachments that are hard to give up.

To sum up, we cling to our life, and it is very difficult to surrender it. So it is also with our attachment to material wealth.

Therefore, if we have unshaken faith in the Three Gems, we are very likely to realize the Dhamma without any striving.

Ye keci, bhikkhave, mayi aveccapasanna sabbe te sotapanna.‡ This means: Those who have unshaken belief in me, the Buddha, are all *sotapanna*.

The above-mentioned individuals are the first type of believers in the Three Gems. There is also a second type of believer. Ninety-one world-cycles ago, there appeared the Buddha Vipassi. During his lifetime the human life-span was very long, about 100,000 years. At that time there was a poor man who had to look after his blind parents. He was very poor and was so busy looking after his parents that he could neither give alms nor observe the Five Precepts; this situation made him very unhappy. Then a monk came to his hut and helped him to take the Refuge and the Five Precepts.

---

* *Dhammapada Atthakatha*, Vol. I, p. 207.
† *Anguttara-Nikaya*, Vol. I, p. 86.
‡ *Anguttara-Nikaya*, Vol. I, p. 351.

When this man died, he was reborn as a deity. For eighty successive lifetimes he became Sakka, King of the Devas. Then he was reborn in the human world and became King of the Four Directions (Universal Monarch) for seventy-five lifetimes. For ninety-one cycles, he became king many times. He was never reborn in the four woeful planes of existence. After numerous wholesome rebirths in wholesome abodes, he was reborn in the days of the Buddha and became an *arahat* at the age of seven. Following the example of the Buddha, this young *arahat* revealed the benefit of taking Refuge in the Three Gems.

There is also a third type of believer, such as the layman named Damila. He was a fisherman his whole life. When he completed his fiftieth year as a fisherman, he became seriously ill and was bedridden. His wife had to nurse him. Then there appeared a monk, and the wife informed her husband of the monk's visit. Davila said, "Tell him throughout fifty years of my life as a fisherman I have not seen him nor has he seen me: I owe him nothing and he owes me nothing."

But the wife was wise and told the monk, "Please, Venerable Sir, accept our homage and our alms." Thereupon the monk asked, "How is the *dayaka* (donor)?" "He is very weak and will not recover from this illness," replied the wife of the sick man.

The monk then went near the man, sat on a plank, and asked, "O *dayaka*, would you like to observe the Precepts?"* "Yes, Venerable Sir," answered the man. Accordingly, the monk began by giving the Refuge first, before giving the Precepts. The man did not live long enough to take Precepts after taking Refuge. As soon as he took the Refuge, he became unconscious and died. He was then reborn as a deity. In that celestial world he reflected, "Why

---

* Precepts are in no sense commandments. They regulate bodily and verbal conduct. The acceptance of the Precepts by the laity is voluntary. See Piyadassi Thera, *Buddhist Meditation* (Kandy, Sri Lanka: Buddhist Publication Society, n.d.), p. 5.

should I be here in the realm of the *devas?*" Then he realized that it was the result of his taking Refuge in the presence of a monk.

As a *deva* he thought, "I owe that monk so much," and further, he thought, "Just by taking the Refuge I was reborn here in this celestial abode. I shall now visit the human world and pay respects to the monk." So he came down to the human world and paid homage to the monk. The monk asked, "Who are you?" "I am Damila, the fisherman. You have done me such a favor by conducting my taking Refuge," said the deity. "Where are you now?" asked the monk. "I am now in the world of *Catu Maharaja* (the lowest of the six heavenly planes). My rebirth there is the result of my taking the Refuge as conducted by you, Venerable Sir. If only I could have lived long enough to take the Precepts also, I would have been born in an even higher plane. Still, I owe you very much, Venerable Sir," said the deity.

Now, if that kind of person can go to the higher planes of existence, let us take the Refuge and surrender ourself to the Buddha, Dhamma, and Sangha.

Once a man from Mandalay named Shwe Oke who was ousted from the Communist Party asked, "Yes, we have to surrender ourselves to the Three Gems—the Buddha, the Dhamma, and the Sangha, but, who is the real Buddha, the real Dhamma, and the real Sangha?" The real Buddha is the one who has all the qualities of the Buddha. So, too, the real Dhamma is the *Lokuttara Dhamma* (supramundane truth) and the real Sangha are those who have attained both the four path-consciousnesses *(magga)* and the four fruit-consciousnesses *(phala)*. So, we need to take Refuge in the real Buddha, the real Dhamma, and the real Sangha. As long as we do not give up contemplation, we will retain the Refuge and be very much benefited. The benefits of *sarana-gamana* are so great that it should be taken for life.

The Sarana-Gamana: Taking of the Refuge for Life

1. *Ajja adim katva aham attanam Buddhassa niyyademi.*
2. *Ajja adim katva aham attanam Dhammassa niyyademi.*
3. *Ajja adim katva aham attaham Sanghassa niyyademi.*
4. *Jivita pariyantikam Buddham saranam gacchami.*
5. *Jivita pariyantikam Dhammam saranam gacchami.*
6. *Jivita pariyantikam Sangham saranam gacchami.**

Recite the above Refuge a second and third time.

The meaning is this:
1. Beginning from today, I offer myself to the Buddha.
2. Beginning from today, I offer myself to the Dhamma.
3. Beginning from today, I offer myself to the Sangha.
4. As long as my life lasts, I go to the Buddha for refuge.
5. As long as my life lasts, I go to the Dhamma for refuge.
6. As long as my life lasts, I go to the Sangha for refuge.

In this connection, it should be noted that the gratitude owed to the one who conducts the taking of Refuge is very great.

There are in the world five classes of benefactors to whom one's gratitude is unlimited. They are the Buddha, the Dhamma, the Sangha, parents, and teachers. Regarding those who belong to the class of teachers we say: *Saranadayaka, sotapatti magga sampapako, arahatto magga-sampapako ti tayo acariya bahu pakarati agata.* That is, he who conducts our taking Refuge, he who helps us to the attainment of the path of *sotapanna*, and he who leads one to the attainment of the *arahat*ship, these three types of teachers are of immeasurable help.

---

* *Digha-Nikaya Atthakatha*, Vol. I, p. 206.

But there are those classes of teachers who, though not listed by the Buddha or his disciples, should still be remembered with gratitude, since they are helpful and wise.

1. The one who conducts ordination, especially the novice ordination.
2. The one who preaches Dhamma, the words of the Buddha.
3. The one who reads out the sacred text during one's ordination.
4. He who leads us to the attainment of *sakadagami* (once-returner—the second stage on the way to *nibbana*).
5. He who leads us to the attainment of *anagami* (never-returner—the third stage on the way to *nibbana*).

Since these five kinds of teachers are of great help, they should be seen as belonging to the class of teachers who should receive our unlimited gratitude.

In conclusion, *sarana-gamana*, the taking of the Refuge, protects us from all dangers and helps us to get rid of any evil nature. Hence, the Refuge should be taken by all, young and old. We must take the Refuge with unshakable faith, otherwise we cannot receive its benefit, no matter who conducts it. With a pure mind, we can take the Refuge in a pagoda, or before a Buddha-*rupa* (image), or in the presence of a *bhikkhu*, or even alone; the most important factors are firm faith and confidence. The Refuge is taken for life. It lasts as long as the person is aware that the Three Gems are the highest, brightest, greatest, and the noblest forces of protection.

Maha Satipatthana Vipassana Insight Meditation

A Discourse by the Most Venerable
Taungpulu Tawya Kaba-Aye Sayadaw
Translated by U Chit Tin and Edited by Sao Htun Hmat Win, 1979

ॐ

May all be blessed with blissful beatitudes!
May our Veneration be to the Almighty, the Most Infallible,
and Auto-Enlightened Supreme Buddha.

O noble yogis! Why do the actions of sentient beings arise? The Buddha expounded that the actions of sentient beings arise because of ignorance and craving. *"Bhikkhus,"* the Buddha said, "this body of the fool comes into existence obstructed by ignorance, and associated with craving."

This body is becoming due to ignorance and craving. So it is most important not to let ignorance arise. Craving does not have a chance to arise when ignorance does not arise. Why? Craving does not arise because there is no ignorance on which craving depends and has a foothold. When craving has ignorance as its foothold, the aggregate of the body in terms of existence is obtained.

Therefore, it is said, "If ignorance is obtained, then the body is obtained." You should meditate in order that ignorance may not arise. Can you?

Sampajana Pabba

The Buddha said:

"*Bhikkhus*, through my physical as well as my intellectual eyes, I do not see any other single thing except the intelligence that can engender the appearance of good *dhammas* (phenomena) that have not yet arisen, and the abandoning of evil *dhammas* that have already arisen. What is that single thing? It is clear comprehension."

In accordance wtih the expositions of the text *Atthasalini*, you must understand all actions clearly.

With regard to *eating:* If a yogi knows eating as eating, knowledge will arise. If the yogi discerns eating while he is eating, then it becomes knowledge. But if he does not know eating as eating discriminately, then it becomes ignorance. It is called ignorance if one does not know what he is doing while he is eating.

With regard to *drinking:* Whenever drinking water or tea or medicine, if he knows drinking as drinking, knowledge will occur. If he does not know this, it will be ignorance.

With regard to *chewing:* Whenever biting edibles such as roots, bulbs, etc., if he knows biting as biting, chewing as chewing, eating as eating, knowledge arises. If he does not know this, then it will be ignorance.

With regard to *licking:* Whenever licking honey, syrup, etc., if he knows licking as licking, knowledge arises. If he does not know this, it will be ignorance.

With regard to *defecating* and *urinating:* Whenever defecating and urinating, if he knows defecating and urinating as defecating and urinating, knowledge arises. If he does not know defecating and urinating as defecating and urinating, it will be ignorance.

With regard to *going:* Whenever the yogi goes, if he knows going as going, knowledge arises. If he does not know this, it will be ignorance.

With regard to *standing:* Whenever he stands, if he knows standing as standing, knowledge arises. If he does not know this, it will be ignorance.

With regard to *sitting:* Whenever he sits, if he knows sitting as sitting, knowledge arises. If he does not know this, it will be ignorance.

With regard to *sleeping:* Whenever he sleeps, if he knows sleeping as sleeping, knowledge arises. If he does not know this, it will be ignorance.

With regard to *awakening:* Whenever he awakes, if he knows awaking as awaking, knowledge arises. If he does not know this, it will be ignorance.

With regard to *talking:* Whenever he talks, if he knows talking as talking, knowledge arises. If he does not know this, it will be ignorance.

With regard to *being silent:* Whenever he remains silent, if he knows remaining silent as remaining silent, knowledge arises. If he does not know this, it will be ignorance.

If he knows this, knowledge arises. If he does not know this, what happens?

"Venerable Sayadaw, if he does not know thus, it will be ignorance."

Oh yes, you are right. Why? Because it is said that ignorance means not knowing. Indeed, you are right. Ignorance, delusion, and not knowing are synonyms. Wisdom, non-delusion, and knowing are synonyms. Not knowing this, what will happen?

"Not knowing this, nothing happens, Venerable Sayadaw."

No, there you miss the point. Not knowing this, does it become ignorance?

"Yes, it does, Venerable Sayadaw."

Well, if ignorance is there, the cyclic law of dependent origination would rotate on as actions, consciousness, mental and physical phenomena, etc., and the span of rebirths will be lengthened. But if he knows this, knowledge will arise; if knowledge arises, ignorance will disappear and cease to be. If ignorance ceases to be, then the cyclic chain of dependent origination—that is, actions, consciousness, mental and physical phenomena, etc.—is cut and the cycle of rebirths stops and does not rotate.

Actions are the effect of ignorance. Thus, the Buddha said, "If there is ignorance as the cause, there are actions as the effect. If there is no ignorance as the cause, there are no actions as the effect. If ignorance ceases, actions cease, too."

Well awake the disciples of Gotama ever arise;
They who by day and by night always concentrate
on the body meditation. (Verse 299)

In brief, all actions done physically, verbally, and mentally must be accepted as the object of contemplation. That is why the Buddha said, *"Bhikkhus,* everything must be known discriminately." In this way, people acquire knowledge. He taught that whenever you are going, it is difficult to continuously know going as going. Though you know, it is difficult to practice. Though you practice, yet it is difficult to accomplish. Why? Because this application of mindfulness, being the object of the Noble Ones, is difficult indeed to practice though it seems easy, and it is quite profound though it may seem shallow. Therefore, the Buddha said, "If there is ignorance as the cause, the actions will arise as the effect. When the cause of ignorance ceases to be, the actions also cease."

It is difficult to differentiate between cause and effect. In order to differentiate between them, let us take the example of a tree and its shadow. The tree becomes first and so it is a cause; the shadow becomes next, and so it is an effect.

Therefore, just as a tree is the cause and the shadow is the effect, so also is ignorance the cause and actions the effect. If there is no ignorance, there will be no actions. But if there is no tree, there is no shadow. If there is a tree then there is a shadow.

That is why the Buddha said, "If there is ignorance, actions arise. If ignorance ceases to be, the actions also cease. Do not think so lightly about the cessation of actions. It is the cessation of an existence, the extinction of an existence, the culmination of a being."

Why? Because there is no ignorance. If there is ignorance, actions arise; that is, the birth of a being will certainly be obtained. "If ignorance is accepted," the Buddha said, "the aggregate-body is obtained."

Therefore, in order to gain knowledge, whenever you see, hear, smell, eat, touch, know, you should contemplate them. Just at the right moment of seeing, contemplate seeing as seeing. Just at the right moment of hearing, contemplate hearing as hearing. Just at the right moment of smelling, contemplate smelling as smelling. Just at the right moment of eating, contemplate eating as eating. Just at the right moment of touching, contemplate touching as touching. Just at the right moment of knowing, contemplate knowing as knowing.

Therefore you should develop your insight meditation in accordance with the teachings of the Buddha. Moreover, you should contemplate whatever actions you are doing: eating, drinking, chewing, licking, sleeping, waking, talking, remaining silent, breathing in, breathing out, rising and falling movements of your abdomen,

hot and cold, soft and hard, subtle and coarse, agreeable and dis-
agreeable feelings, being greedy, feeling hatred, delusion, conceit, envy, selfishness, anger, bearing a grudge, besmirching, wishing
to discredit, wishing to debase, concealing fault, hypocrisy, feeling
mental rigidity, rivalry, sorrow, lamentation, pain, grief, etc. There
are many things which you should contemplate; the more you contemplate the more you will gain knowledge.

When knowledge arises, ignorance ceases. When ignorance
ceases there is no more birth. It is culminated. The Buddha said,
"Actions never cease due to any other cause but from the cessation
of ignorance." Why? Because as the Buddha said, "Actions cease
only when ignorance ceases. All evil has ignorance as its forerunner."

Therefore, the Buddha said, *"Bhikkhus,* for the commitment of
evil *dhammas,* ignorance is the forerunner. If ignorance, the root
of all defilements, is cut off, all defilements will be well uprooted."

Then by which means must ignorance be cut off? Ignorance
must be cut off by means of mindful contemplation. Mindful
contemplation itself is knowledge. If knowledge arises, ignorance
cannot exist. Therefore, the Buddha said, "As soon as knowledge
arises, it must be understood that ignorance is dispelled. If ignorance is dispelled, not a single defilement, whatever it may be,
can arise."

If there is no defilement and if the defilement does not arise,
nothing can yield the condition of birth. The Buddha said, "Action
without defilement cannot produce the condition of birth."

It should be noted here that "action without defilement" means
good action. Good action does not produce a new birth; on the
contrary, it extinguishes the existence. It has no defilement. Only
evil action produces a new birth. Even then all evil actions do
not produce elements of birth. Only craving creates a new birth.
Therefore, the Buddha said, "Evil *dhammas* means twelve types
of evil consciousness. Of them, craving especially is the strongest

evil dhamma. It is indeed able to create new birth, and therefore it is called *panobhavika.*"

Only craving is the evil thing which creates a new birth. In brief, the state of craving and of being excited is called *kamma*-action. Therefore the Buddha said, "In order to stop rebirth in the next existence, whenever an action is done physically, verbally, or mentally, if you contemplate each of them once with good intention, you know that a rebirth is cut off." The aforementioned *kamma*-action without defilement means not only mind development, but also practicing charity and good morality. Charity and morality should not be misunderstood as the cause of prolonging the cycle of rebirths. Just to suggest a hint that charity and morality are not causes which prolong the cycle of rebirths, let me quote an extract from the Pali Canon which describes the three root-causes of unwholesome actions and the three root-causes of wholesome actions. The Buddha said, "O monks, greed, hatred, and delusion are the three root-causes of evil actions. Non-greed, non-hatred, and non-delusion are the three root-causes of good actions. The three evil root-causes produce *kamma*-action; but they do not stop *kamma*-action. The three good root-causes stop *kamma*-action but they do not produce *kamma*-action."

Therefore, the Buddha said, "O monks, there is a certain *kamma*-action that leads to the cycle of suffering, which is produced by greed, which is caused by greed, which has greed as its root-cause, which has greed as the root-cause of arising. That *kamma*-action which leads to the cycle of suffering is called bad *kamma*-action. That bad *kamma*-action is faulty. That bad *kamma*-action yields a bad result. That bad *kamma*-action which leads to the cycle of suffering produces the arising of *kamma*-action. That bad *kamma*-action does not make *kamma*-action cease." The meaning is the same with regard to hatred and delusion. This is to show how *kamma*-action is produced and how it is not culminated.

How Kamma-action Ceases

The Buddha said: *"Bhikkhus,* there is a certain *kamma*-action that leads to *nibbana,* the cessation of suffering, which is produced by non-greed, which is caused by non-greed, which has non-greed as its root-cause, which has non-greed as the root-cause of arising. That *kamma*-action which leads to *nibbana,* the cessation of suffering, is called good *kamma*-action. That good action is faultless. That good action yields a good result. That good action makes *kamma*-action cease. That good action does not produce the arising of *kamma*-action."

The Buddha explained in another way that good action does not produce *kamma*-action, and that it does lead to the cessation of *kamma*-action. The Buddha expounded thus: "Non-greed is at the root of charity, non-hatred is at the root of morality, and non-delusion is at the root of mental development."

Let me explain the fact that the three good actions—charity, morality, and mental development—do not engender the cyclic rotation of rebirths, but instead they cut it off.

The Transcendental Path and Transcendental Fruition cannot be attained without depending on something. On what do they depend? They have to depend on charity, morality, and mental development. Depending only on these three things, the Paths and Fruitions can surely be attained. However, good actions depending on charity and morality are too weak to generate higher results; only the lower three Transcendental Paths and Transcendental Fruitions can be attained. Whereas good actions depending on mental development are so powerful that the highest Transcendental Path and the highest Transcendental Fruition can be attained.

Therefore, the Buddha said, "Charity and morality, being feeble, can lead to the state of streamwinner; they can also lead to the state of once-returner; so also to the state of never-returner. Mental development, being powerful, will lead to the state of *arahat-ship.*"

Understanding the Appearing and Disappearing of Defilements

Try to understand the appearing and disappearing of defilements in accordance with the following statements:

1. The appearing of defilements in the eye:
   a) When I see what I want to see, then greed does arise;
   b) When I see what I do not want to see, then hatred does arise;
   c) When I do not know what I want to see, then ignorance does arise;
   d) When I do not know what I do not want to see, then ignorance does arise.

   Dispelling defilements in the eye:
   e) When I know what I want to see, then knowledge does arise;
   f) When I know what I do not want to see, then knowledge does arise.

2. The appearing of defilements in the ear:
   a) When I hear what I want to hear, then greed does arise;
   b) When I hear what I do not want to hear, then hatred does arise;
   c) When I do not know what I want to hear, then ignorance does arise;
   d) When I do not know what I do not want to hear, then ignorance does arise.

Dispelling defilements in the ear:
e) When I know what I want to hear, then knowledge does arise;
f) When I know what I do not want to hear, then knowledge does arise.

3. The appearing of defilements in the nose:
   a) When I smell what I want to smell, then greed does arise;
   b) When I smell what I do not want to smell, then hatred does arise;
   c) When I do not know what I want to smell, then ignorance does arise;
   d) When I do not know what I do not want to smell, then ignorance does arise.

Dispelling defilements in the nose:
e) When I know what I want to smell, then knowledge does arise;
f) When I know what I don't want to smell, then knowledge does arise.

4. The appearing of defilements at the tongue:
   a) When I taste what I want to taste, then greed does arise;
   b) When I taste what I do not want to taste, then hatred does arise;
   c) When I do not know what I want to taste, then ignorance does arise;
   d) When I do not know what I do not want to taste, then ignorance does arise.

Dispelling defilements at the tongue:
e) When I know what I want to taste, then knowledge does arise;

f) When I know what I don't want to taste, then knowledge does arise.

5. The appearing of defilements in the body:
   a) When I touch what I want to touch, then greed does arise;
   b) When I touch what I do not want to touch, then hatred does arise;
   c) When I do not know what I want to touch, then ignorance does arise;
   d) When I do not know what I do not want to touch, then ignorance does arise.

   Dispelling defilements of the body:
   e) When I know what I want to touch, then knowledge does arise;
   f) When I know what I don't want to touch, then knowledge does arise.

6. The appearing of defilements in the mind:
   a) When I know what I want to know, then greed does arise;
   b) When I know what I do not want to know, then hatred does arise;
   c) When I do not know what I want to know, then ignorance does arise;
   d) When I do not know what I do not want to know, then ignorance does arise.

   Dispelling defilements at the mind:
   e) When I know what I want to know, then knowledge does arise;
   f) When I know what I don't want to know, then knowledge does arise.

Whatever actions you are doing, such as moving, standing, sitting, lying, etc., contemplate in like manner as described above. "Actions" means all actions done physically, verbally, that is, all actions which necessarily should be done.

There is an old saying of the virtuous: "Do not stay heedlessly while performing actions. There are always actions; whatever you are doing they are all actions; but you are heedless, i.e., you forget to contemplate them. If you can contemplate them as much as possible, you will gain knowledge which will lead to the cessation of the cycle of rebirths. If you cannot contemplate in this way, you will be in ignorance which will keep you in the cycle of rebirths.

Therefore the wise men said, "Not knowing means ignorance; knowing means knowledge; these two things must lucidly be distinguished. Through ignorance the chain of dependent origination rotates. But through knowledge, the chain is cut."

Samatha and Vipassana Meditation

Contemplation on the body is called calming meditation *(samatha)*; clear comprehension is called insight meditation *(vipassana)*. Put another way, the tranquilizing of defilements is called calming meditation. Various types of contemplating and meditating on the true nature of mind and matter are called insight meditations.

The Ultimate and Conventional Truths

1. "I," "he," "man," "woman," etc. are all conventional truths.
2. Seeing, hearing, smelling, eating, contacting, knowing, etc., are ultimate truths.

A maxim about this is, "Realizing that it is not "I," but only mind-and-matter, is the ultimate truth.

Nama-rupa-pariccheda Nana

Knowing discriminately mind and matter, as such-and-such is mind, and such-and-such is matter, is called *nama-rupa-pariccheda nana*. Though you may be a common layperson, if you discern mind and matter, you can keep yourself free from the four obstacles for a moment. Being well emancipated as an *arahat* you live happily for a moment. Here is the reference: "If a yogi contemplates and realizes thus: 'This mind-and-matter is not I, it is only mind-and-matter. This mind-and-matter is not my soul, not my self, it is only mind-and-matter," he has no grasping by craving, conceit, and wrong view, and his mind is well emancipated from the four obstacles.

Though you may be an ordinary layperson, if you really discern mind-and-matter, you can live happily as an *arahat* who has extinguished the four biases. But if you are an ordinary yogi you can overcome the four biases only for a moment.

Three Kinds of Knowledge Discerning Mind-and-Matter

There are three kinds of knowledge discerning mind-and-matter, namely:
1. Knowledge acquired through hearing or learning;
2. Knowledge acquired through thinking;
3. Knowledge acquired through developmental practices or insight meditation.

Of these three, realizing mind-and-matter through hearing-knowledge or through thinking-knowledge is not a bona fide realization. Realizing mind-and-matter through developmental practices or insight contemplation is said to be a perfect realization.

How to Contemplate to Discern Mind-and-Matter Easily

The wish to go is the mind but it is the matter that goes. Only when the mind wants to go does the matter then go. If the mind does not want to go, the matter will not go.
A verse maxim:

1. The wish to go is mind,
   The thing that goes is matter.
   The thing that goes is not
   A person, a being,
   Neither another, a person, nor I,
   Neither man nor woman,
   Nor soul, nor ego.
   Only mind-and-matter goes;
   Only mind-and-matter goes.

2. The wish to stand is mind,
   The thing that stands is matter.
   The thing that stands is not
   A person, a being,
   Neither another, a person, nor I,
   Neither man nor woman,
   Nor soul, nor ego.
   Only mind-and-matter stands;
   Only mind-and-matter stands.

3. The wish to sit is mind,
   The thing that sits is matter.
   The thing that sits is not
   A person, a being,
   Neither another, a person, nor I,
   Neither man nor woman,

Nor soul, nor ego.
Only mind-and-matter sits;
Only mind-and-matter sits.

4. The wish to sleep is mind,
   The thing that sleeps is matter.
   The thing that sleeps is not
   A person, a being,
   Neither another, a person, nor I,
   Neither man nor woman,
   Nor soul, nor ego.
   Only mind-and-matter sleeps;
   Only mind-and-matter sleeps.

Only the four postures, namely, going, standing, sitting, sleeping, are described here. The other activities should also be contemplated in like manner.

Buying, selling, farming, cultivating, watering, weeding, ploughing, sewing, extracting plants, transplanting, reaping grass, cutting grass into pieces, plucking cotton, carding cotton, cleaning cotton, spinning thread, sizing thread, setting thread, dying, designing, arranging thread for looms, weaving, cooking, pounding rice, plucking vegetables, cutting vegetables, gathering kindling, carrying water, and all other activities should be done with mindfulness and care, contemplated with great caution and diligence.

If mind-and-matter are truly realized, you will not be obsessed by the sixty-two kinds of wrong views. Thus it is said, "If mind-and-matter are discriminately recognized and realized, the yogi does not cling to the view of personal attachment but abandons it, and thus gains the purity of views."

The True Realization of Mind-and-Matter

If a yogi discerns mind-and-matter, he does not see a man or a woman. Through his developing insight knowledge of contemplation, the yogi will realize thus: "Just as a wooden doll does not lose its original form, still, it is neither a real man nor a woman." If the yogi's insight knowledge is pure, though the yogi may be just an average person, he or she will be much benefited. All sufferings will cease, and consequently the yogi will live happily. The stronger personal attachment is, the greater will be the suffering.

Three Kinds of Insight Knowledge
That Yield Especially Abundant Benefit

There are three kinds, namely:

1. The knowledge of the true nature of reality. This means, in the ultimate sense, the insight knowledge which realizes that there is only mind-and-matter in the thirty-one spheres of existence of beings; there is nothing else except mind-and-matter.

2. The knowledge of right views. This means the realization that there is neither "he" nor "I," neither "man" nor "woman," etc. as the doer of *kamma*-actions; there is neither he nor I, neither man nor woman, etc. as one who enjoys the results of *kamma*-actions. This knowledge knows only two things, mind and matter.

3. The knowledge of transcending all skeptical doubts. This means the overcoming of all skeptical doubts about living things such as person, being, I, he, man, woman, human, deity, animal, ghost; they are nothing but mind and matter in various forms and appearances.

Regarding non-living things as well, the yogi has no skeptical doubts. He knows that a pot, a house, wood, bamboo, brick, stone, gold, silver, the sun, the moon, water, earth, ocean, jungle, mountain, etc. are only matter in various forms and appearance. Thus he transcends all skeptical doubts.

These three insight-knowledges are different in terms, but they are all the same in meaning.

Therefore it is said, "When a yogi practicing insight meditation possesses this knowledge, he obtains comfort as well as a foothold in the teachings of the Buddha, he is now certain of his meaningful existence; he is to be named a junior streamwinner."

If he realizes the becoming and vanishing of both mind and matter, even though he may live for only a day, he is nobler than the one who survives him for a century.

The becoming and vanishing of mind and matter are not only speculation. They are real objects of direct knowledge. Neither mind nor matter alone can happen independently but are possible only when both mind and matter cooperate with each other.

The Becoming and Vanishing of Mind and Matter

It can be said that contemplation itself is becoming. On every contemplation mind and matter become and vanish subsequently.

Where do the becoming and vanishing take place?

1. They become and vanish in the eyes.
2. They become and vanish in the ears.
3. They become and vanish in the nose.
4. They become and vanish on the tongue.
5. They become and vanish in the body.
6. They become and vanish in the heart.

In other words,

     a) Contemplation on seeing as "seeing-seeing" is the becoming. On every contemplation of seeing, mind-and-matter become and consequently they vanish.

b) Contemplation on hearing as "hearing-hearing" is the becoming. On every contemplation of hearing, mind-and-matter become and consequently they vanish.

c) Contemplation on smelling as "smelling-smelling" is the becoming. On every contemplation of smelling, mind-and-matter become and consequently they vanish.

d) Contemplation on eating as "eating-eating" is the becoming. On every contemplation of eating, mind-and-matter become and consequently they vanish.

e) Contemplation on touching as "touching-touching" is the becoming. On every contemplation of touching, mind-and-matter become and consequently they vanish.

f) Contemplation on knowing as "knowing-knowing" is the becoming. On every contemplation of knowing, mind-and-matter become and consequently they vanish.

Therefore the Buddha taught, "If one does not realize the becoming and vanishing of mind and matter, even though he may live for a century, he is not worthy of living. If he realizes the becoming and vanishing of mind-and-matter, even though he lives for a day, he is much nobler than the one who lives a hundred years without realizing them."

O yogis, you must continuously and intensively contemplate on mind and matter and develop your knowledge. I am sure you will be much benefited. If you develop your wisdom more and more, even if you develop wisdom only for a moment, you are nobler than the one who lives a hundred years without realizing this.

How long is a moment? The time for ten snappings of the fingers is called a moment.

A moment is equal to the time of ten snappings of the fingers. Ten moments may be equal to a minute. If a yogi contemplates for a minute, he is nobler than the one who lives for a hundred years without realizing mind-and-matter.

A person who strenuously practices the Dhamma and lives only for a moment is nobler than someone who is too bored to practice the Dhamma and indolently lives for a hundred years.

As the Buddha admonished: "Now, while you are sitting, do not let your mind wander about; close your eyes, concentrate, and contemplate on sitting as "sitting-sitting." If you contemplate even for a minute, you will be nobler than the one who lives a thousand years without realizing mind-and-matter."

Five Directives

The two things to be discriminately comprehended:

1. Two things, namely mind and matter, must be discriminately comprehended.

The two things to be abandoned:

2. Two things, namely ignorance and craving for existence, must be abandoned.

The two things to be developed:

3. Two things, namely concentration and insight meditation, must be developed.

That to be attained is *Nibbana:*

a) Of these two, if concentration is developed, matter is discriminately comprehended. If matter is discriminately comprehended, craving is abandoned. If craving is abandoned, the yogi overcomes lust and so confronts the emancipation of mind from the defilements.

    b) If insight meditation be developed, mind is thoroughly comprehended. If mind be thoroughly comprehended, ignorance is abandoned.

If ignorance is abandoned, the yogi overcomes lust and so attains the emancipation of knowledge from the defilements. Discerning merely mind and matter, he or she will abandon the view of selfish personal attachments; and contemplating emphatically upon selflessness, he or she becomes disgusted by suffering and will successively reach enlightenment and put an end to suffering.

Two kinds of diseases of a being:

    4. There are two kinds of diseases of a being, namely ignorance and craving for existence.

    a) The medicine to cure the disease of craving is concentration of mind.

    b) The medicine to cure the disease of ignorance is insight meditation.

Through the practice of the foundations of mindfulness, both the yogi and others are said to be well protected:

    5. The foundations of mindfulness must be practiced to protect yourself. And the foundations of mindfulness must be practiced to protect others.

    a) If you yourself are protected, others are also guarded.

    b) If others are guarded, you yourself are protected, too. Thus it should be understood.

Thirty-two Parts
of the Body Meditation

ॐ

According to the Venerable Taungpulu Sayadaw, contemplation on the thirty-two parts of the body as referred to in early Buddhist literature, both canonical and non-canonical, has immense benefits. In the first place, you will acquire a calm mind and body just by turning your attention to the parts of the body. You can achieve very good concentration by methodically repeating and visualizing the various parts of the body, and you can even heal yourself of different diseases by concentrating on affected organs. If you practice the meditation on a regular basis, you can experience the Four Noble Truths and eventually attain enlightenment. As the Buddha said to the *deva* Rohita,

> Oh, Rohita Nat! I do not preach that the cessation of the world of suffering could be done without the attainment of *Nibbana*. Within this fathom-long body, with its thoughts and emotions, I declare the world, the origin of the world, the cessation of the world, and the path leading to the cessation of the world.*

The Buddha refers to the thirty-two parts of the body in several of his discourses and emphasizes the importance of taking up these parts as an object of meditation. The benefits of this meditation are so powerful that Taungpulu Sayadaw considered it a core teaching of the Buddha; the Sayadaw created a method of

---

* *Samyutta Nikaya, Nanatittiya Vagga, Rohitassa Sutta.*

recitation and visualization out of his own experience which can be completed in 165 days (or in one hour if you chant all the groups in one sitting).

Even if you can remember only one line—just five parts—in your daily practice, please try to repeat and visualize them until you can see them as clearly as you see your five fingers. This will guarantee you progress in your mindfulness practice, and you will be able to get in touch with your priceless vehicle, the body, in a very direct way.

I

1. Hair of the Head, Hair of the Body, Nails, Teeth, Skin.
   Forward five days

2. Skin, Teeth, Nails, Hair of the Body, Hair of the Head.
   Backward five days

3. Hair of the Head, Hair of the Body, Nails, Teeth, Skin;
   Skin, Teeth, Nails, Hair of the Body, Hair of the Head.
   Forward and Backward five days

II

(Hair of the Head, Hair of the Body, Nails, Teeth, Skin)

4. Flesh, Sinews, Bones, Bone Marrow, Kidney.
   Forward five days

5. Kidney, Bone Marrow, Bones, Sinews, Flesh.
   Backward five days

6. Flesh, Sinews, Bones, Bone Marrow, Kidney;
   Kidney, Bone Marrow, Bones, Sinews, Flesh.
   Forward and Backward five days

(Skin, Teeth, Nails, Hair of the Body, Hair of the Head)

7. Hair of the Head, Hair of the Body, Nails, Teeth, Skin,
   Flesh, Sinews, Bones, Bone Marrow, Kidney.
   Forward five days

8. Kidney, Bone Marrow, Bones, Sinews, Flesh, Skin, Teeth,
   Nails, Hair of the Body, Hair of the Head.
   Backward five days

9. Hair of the Head, Hair of the Body, Nails, Teeth, Skin,
   Flesh, Sinews, Bones, Bone Marrow, Kidney;
   Kidney, Bone Marrow, Bones, Sinews, Flesh, Skin, Teeth,
   Nails, Hair of the Body, Hair of the Head.
   Forward and Backward five days

III

(Hair of the Body, Hair of the Head, Nails, Teeth, Skin,
Flesh, Sinews, Bones, Bone Marrow, Kidney)

10. Heart, Liver, Diaphragm, Spleen, Lungs.
    Forward five days

11. Lungs, Spleen, Diaphragm, Liver, Heart.
    Backward five days

12. Heart, Liver, Diaphragm, Spleen, Lungs;
    Lungs, Spleen, Diaphragm, Liver, Heart.
    Forward and Backward five days

    (Kidney, Bone Marrow, Bones, Sinews, Flesh, Skin, Teeth,
    Nails, Hair of the Body, Hair of the Head)

13. Hair of the Head, Hair of the Body, Nails, Teeth, Skin,
    Flesh, Sinews, Bones, Bone Marrow, Kidney, Heart, Liver,
    Diaphragm, Spleen, Lungs.
    Forward five days

14. Lungs, Spleen, Diaphragm, Liver, Heart, Kidney, Bone
    Marrow, Bones, Sinews, Flesh, Skin, Teeth, Nails, Hair of
    the Body, Hair of the Head.
    Backward five days

15. Hair of the Head, Hair of the Body, Nails, Teeth, Skin,
    Flesh, Sinews, Bones, Bone Marrow, Kidney, Heart, Liver,
    Diaphragm, Spleen, Lungs;
    Lungs, Spleen, Diaphragm, Liver, Heart, Kidney, Bone
    Marrow, Bones, Sinews, Flesh, Skin, Teeth, Nails, Hair of
    the Body, Hair of the Head.
    Forward and Backward five days

IV

(Hair of the Head, Hair of the Body, Nails, Teeth, Skin,
Flesh, Sinews, Bones, Bone Marrow, Kidney, Heart, Liver,
Diaphragm, Spleen, Lungs)

16. Bowels, Intestines, Mesentery, Feces, Brain.
    Forward five days

17. Brain, Feces, Mesentery, Intestines, Bowels.
    Backward five days

18. Bowels, Intestines, Mesentery, Feces, Brain;
    Brain, Feces, Mesentery, Intestines, Bowels.
    Forward and Backward five days

    (Lungs, Spleen, Membrane, Liver, Heart, Kidney, Bone
    Marrow, Bones, Sinews, Flesh, Skin, Teeth, Nails, Hair of
    the Body, Hair of the Head)

19. Hair of the Head, Hair of the Body, Nails, Teeth, Skin,
    Flesh, Sinews, Bones, Bone Marrow, Kidney, Heart, Liver,
    Diaphragm, Spleen, Lungs, Bowels, Intestines, Mesentery,
    Feces, Brain.
    Forward five days

20. Brain, Feces, Mesentery, Intestines, Bowels, Lungs, Spleen, Diaphragm, Liver, Heart, Kidney, Bone Marrow, Bones, Sinews, Flesh, Skin, Teeth, Nails, Hair of the Body, Hair of the Head.
Backward five days

21. Hair of the Head, Hair of the Body, Nails, Teeth, Skin, Flesh, Sinews, Bones, Bone Marrow, Kidney, Heart, Liver, Diaphragm, Spleen, Lungs, Bowels, Intestines, Mesentery, Feces, Brain;
Brain, Feces, Mesentery, Intestines, Bowels, Lungs, Spleen, Diaphragm, Liver, Heart, Kidney, Bone Marrow, Bones, Sinews, Flesh, Skin, Teeth, Nails, Hair of the Body, Hair of the Head.
Forward and Backward five days

V

(Hair of the Head, Hair of the Body, Nails, Teeth, Skin, Flesh, Sinews, Bones, Bone Marrow, Kidney, Heart, Liver, Diaphragm, Spleen, Lungs, Bowels, Intestines, Mesentery, Feces, Brain)

22. Bile, Phlegm, Pus, Blood, Sweat, Solid Fat.
Foward five days

23. Solid Fat, Sweat, Blood, Pus, Phlegm, Bile.
Backward five days

24. Bile, Phlegm, Pus, Blood, Sweat, Solid Fat;
Solid Fat, Sweat, Blood, Pus, Phlegm, Bile.
Forward and Backward five days

(Brain, Feces, Mesentery, Intestines, Bowels, Lungs, Spleen, Diaphragm, Liver, Heart, Kidney, Bone Marrow, Bones, Sinews, Flesh, Skin, Teeth, Nails, Hair of the Body, Hair of the Head)

25. Hair of the Head, Hair of the Body, Nails, Teeth, Skin, Flesh, Sinews, Bones, Bone Marrow, Kidney, Heart, Liver, Diaphragm, Spleen, Lungs, Bowels, Intestines, Mesentery, Feces, Brain, Bile, Phlegm, Pus, Blood, Sweat, Solid Fat. *Forward five days*

26. Solid Fat, Sweat, Blood, Pus, Phlegm, Bile, Brain, Feces, Mesentery, Intestines, Bowels, Lungs, Spleen, Diaphragm, Liver, Heart, Kidney, Bone Marrow, Bones, Sinews, Flesh, Skin, Teeth, Nails, Hair of the Body, Hair of the Head. *Backward five days*

27. Hair of the Head, Hair of the Body, Nails, Teeth, Skin, Flesh, Sinews, Bones, Bone Marrow, Kidney, Heart, Liver, Diaphragm, Spleen, Lungs, Bowels, Intestines, Mesentery, Feces, Brain, Bile, Phlegm, Pus, Blood, Sweat, Solid Fat; Solid Fat, Sweat, Blood, Pus, Phlegm, Bile, Brain, Feces, Mesentery, Intestines, Bowels, Lungs, Spleen, Diaphragm, Liver, Heart, Kidney, Bone Marrow, Bones, Sinews, Flesh, Skin, Teeth, Nails, Hair of the Body, Hair of the Head. *Foward and Backward five days*

VI

(Hair of the Head, Hair of the Body, Nails, Teeth, Skin, Flesh, Sinews, Bones, Bone Marrow, Kidney, Heart, Liver, Diaphragm, Spleen, Lungs, Bowels, Intestine, Mesentery, Feces, Brain, Bile, Phlegm, Pus, Blood, Sweat, Solid Fat)

28. Tears, Liquid Fat, Saliva, Mucus, Synovic Fluid, Urine. *Forward five days*

29. Urine, Synovic Fluid, Mucus, Saliva, Liquid Fat, Tears. *Backward five days*

30. Tears, Liquid Fat, Saliva, Mucus, Synovic Fluid, Urine; Urine, Synovic Fluid, Mucus, Saliva, Liquid Fat, Tears. *Forward and Backward five days*

(Solid Fat, Sweat, Pus, Blood, Phlegm, Bile, Brain, Feces, Mesentery, Intestines, Bowels, Lungs, Spleen, Diaphragm, Liver, Heart, Kidney, Bone Marrow, Bones, Sinews, Flesh, Skin, Teeth, Nails, Hair of the Body, Hair of the Head)

31. Hair of the Head, Hair of the Body, Nails, Teeth, Skin, Flesh, Sinews, Bones, Bone Marrow, Kidney, Heart, Liver, Diaphragm, Spleen, Lungs, Bowels, Intestines, Mesentery, Feces, Brain, Bile, Phlegm, Pus, Blood, Sweat, Solid Fat, Tears, Liquid Fat, Saliva, Mucus, Synovic Fluid, Urine. *Forward five days*

32. Urine, Synovic Fluid, Mucus, Saliva, Liquid Fat, Tears, Solid Fat, Sweat, Blood, Pus, Phlegm, Bile, Brain, Feces, Mesentery, Intestines, Bowels, Lungs, Spleen, Diaphragm, Liver, Heart, Kidney, Bone Marrow, Bones, Sinews, Flesh, Skin, Teeth, Nails, Hair of the Body, Hair of the Head. *Backward five days*

33. Hair of the Head, Hair of the Body, Nails, Teeth, Skin, Flesh, Sinews, Bones, Bone Marrow, Kidney, Heart, Liver, Diaphragm, Spleen, Lungs, Bowels, Intestines, Mesentery, Feces, Brain, Bile, Phlegm, Pus, Blood, Sweat, Solid Fat, Tears, Liquid Fat, Saliva, Mucus, Synovic Fluid, Urine; Urine, Synovic Fluid, Mucus, Saliva, Liquid Fat, Tears, Solid Fat, Sweat, Blood, Pus, Phlegm, Bile, Brain, Feces, Mesentery, Intestines, Bowels, Lungs, Spleen, Diaphragm, Liver, Heart, Kidney, Bone Marrow, Bones, Sinews, Flesh, Skin, Teeth, Nails, Hair of the Body, Hair of the Head. *Forward and Backward five days*

ᴣ